Eight Essential Elements to Employment

The path to employment, recruitment & consulting success

Pauline Visser

First published by Busybird Publishing 2017
Copyright © 2017 Pauline Visser

ISBN
Print: 978-1-925692-19-8
Ebook: 978-1-925692-32-7

Pauline Visser has asserted her right under the Copyright, Designs and Patents Act 1988 to be identified as the author of this work. The information in this book is based on the author's experiences and opinions. The publisher specifically disclaims responsibility for any adverse consequences, which may result from use of the information contained herein. Permission to use information has been sought by the author. Any breaches will be rectified in further editions of the book.

All rights reserved. No part of this publication may be reproduced, stored in or introduced into a retrieval system, or transmitted in any form, or by any means (electronic, mechanical, photocopying, recording or otherwise) without the prior written permission of the author. Any person who does any unauthorised act in relation to this publication may be liable to criminal prosecution and civil claims for damages. Enquiries should be made through the publisher.

Cover image: Ishika Rai
Cover design: Kev Howlett, Busybird
Layout and typesetting: Busybird Publishing:

Busybird Publishing
2/118 Para Road
Montmorency, Victoria
Australia 3094
www.busybird.com.au

Dedication

This book is dedicated to those seeking the right path for themselves or others. May your journey be rewarding and successful!

Contents

Foreword	i
About the Author	iii
Introduction	xi
Illustrator/Artist	xiii
SECTION 1. The Customers	**1**
The Individual	3
The Business Professional	10
The Consultant	24
SECTION 2. The Elements	**37**
The Eight Essential Elements to Employment	39
SECTION 3. The Chapters	**41**
Structure of each chapter	43
1. Motivate Yourself	45
2. Present Yourself	53
3. Upskill Yourself	65
4. Amazing Application	79
5. Rocking Resume	93
6. Pre Interview	111
7. In Interview	123
8. Post Interview	135
SECTION 4. The Lists	**147**
SECTION 5. The Next Step	**157**

Foreword

Here's a HOW-TO book that's actually written by a 'subject matter expert' with years of hands-on experience in every aspect of the employment spectrum. Pauline knows what she's talking about.

When it comes to advice for job seekers, far too many self-help books are written by career management advisors and workplace psychologists, who know a lot about organisational psychology, career development and advancement, personal branding and marketing but very little about how to break into the job market for the average job seeker.

And for employers without the expertise of an in-house HR department to do the recruiting job for them, and the recruitment consultants striving to place candidates in jobs where they'll thrive and succeed, this book is an invaluable tool for the strategies and processes essential for a successful hiring results.

I'm delighted that Pauline Visser has finally given job seekers, employers and recruiters a meaningful, practical, easy-to-follow set of instructions that will empower them with the know-how to manage their part in the world of work successfully.

Eight Essential Elements to Employment

I've known Pauline for over 20 years during which time she has amassed an enormous body of job-search and recruitment experience.

With a career that includes in-house recruiting for large and small companies, working in the state and federal government job-placement and skills training sector, the commercial agency recruitment industry and her own business as an employment coach and HR consultant she has been able to create a tool to draw from that is as practical as it is valuable.

Lyn Cairns – Director

About the Author

It was a grey winter's day in July 1996. She was 37 and had two girls under 4 when she experienced a dramatic wake-up call. Her feet went numb! Then the altered sensation took off like a train without a driver and rapidly progressed up through her body with no signs of stopping.

Her life took a major turn when the neurologist told her to take care when carrying her 15-month-old daughter around in case her legs gave way from under her. The numb sensation had progressed quickly up from the soles of her feet to just above her waist. The MRI was done as a diagnostic test and, after receiving two bags of an infusion to treat the inflammation that had been detected in her spinal cord, she was discharged from hospital and advised to go home and *"get on with life"*.

Pauline seriously wondered how she was going to do that.

She didn't know if these frightening symptoms would dissipate and apparently the neurologist didn't either. With no change in her condition, or any guarantees in sight, she was sent home to begin living this *new life*. She soon realised that positivity would become her new best friend.

Over the following eight weeks, the numbness gradually drained from her body, but *never* really left the soles of her feet.

It was perhaps a lucky thing that she happened to be on a break from her all-consuming and demanding career of recruiting while she raised her two children to school age, because over the following five years, she clawed her way through the stages of grief while learning to accept her *new life* and its many restrictions. She journeyed through denial, anger, bargaining, depression, until she eventually made it to acceptance. Over that time she read anything relevant, researched, networked and made connections. Working on the philosophy that knowledge is power, she became very powerful.

Pauline's new reality was that she was living with Multiple Sclerosis (MS).

One day she turned the radio on and heard the words *"you need to help people"*, followed by a silence, as if for emphasis. The reception dropped out momentarily, long enough for the message to resonate clearly. Whatever the reason for this message, she *got* it!

She had already been planning her return to the workforce after a 7-year hiatus. She was finally ready, having accepted her restrictions and adjusting to her new lifestyle. She had loved recruiting but felt it was time for a change of direction, so her sights were set on becoming a Case Manager for long-term unemployed clients.

Following the process that is outlined in the *Eight Essential Elements to Employment*, she applied for the first suitable role she saw advertised. It became apparent during the conversations with the employer that this was not the environment she was seeking. The interview then became part of her research for the next role. It gave her ideas on how to select and apply for the right job and so she adjusted her search target and rejoined the market.

The second job she applied for (after a 7-year break and in a new field) was hers!

She thoroughly enjoyed this job but in 2013, no longer able to work full-time in a demanding and high-stress environment, she set up her own business: **Pauline Visser Employment Coaching**. The joys of technology allowed her to work from anywhere and be flexible enough to work only in times of peak energy and clarity and be kind to herself when her body required it. This style of business became her new reality. It was during this period that she had the opportunity to participate in a Writer's Retreat run by Jo Johnson – The Content Coach. This is when she finally realised that the information that was spinning around in her head, that had taken her many years to gather, was actually highly valuable and could benefit others if packaged correctly.

Jo effortlessly condensed the information Pauline provided her with and made sense of it. *"Yes"*, she said, as she drew a diagram of Pauline's business taking shape before her. *"You can definitely build a solid business from your ideas and experience; you just need to focus them, refine the offerings, and be absolutely clear about who you can help".* The result was a description of her three perfect clients and an awakening in her of how valuable the information she held inside was for others.

Eight Essential Elements to Employment is the result.

This book is one of the tools of Pauline's business and represents an outpouring of the knowledge, learnings, experiences and wisdom gained over the preceding thirty years of her career. Together with the know-how of experts in her network, she offers you everything you need to know to be well ahead of your competition in the employment game.

Testimonial

"It is inspiring how many lives have changed as a consequence of working with Pauline. Learning how her experience in Employment Coaching has impacted on her clients is a testament to her passion and expertise in the field".
    Jo Johnson – The Content Coach

Relevant employment history:

Deloitte Haskins & Sells (Moorabbin)	• Introduced HR services to audit clients • Introduced temporary staff service • Developed clients specifically for HR services
McCoy & Associates (Headhunted for role) (Mt. Eliza)	• Planned, marketed and set-up this new recruitment agency • Designed business cards • Advertised and interviewed candidates for talent bank
Personal Choice (South Yarra)	• Recruited admin and clerical staff
Nursing Agency (Mornington)	• Took bookings for medical personnel • Booked nurses into hospital/nursing home shifts

Personnel Unlimited (Mt Eliza)
 	
CO_2 Australia
PP&WCMA
	• Ran this agency in the owner's absence
	• Temporary assignments
	   a) Writing Human Resources (HR) Manual
	   b) Reviewing, updating and initiating new Policies

Philip Morris Ltd. (Moorabbin – Australian HO)	• Recruited, tested and inducted staff • Supported interstate offices in recruitment • Travelled to NSW, SA & NT to assist State Managers • Trained Managers in Recruitment • On panel to select tertiary students for work experience

About the Author

Western Staff (Moorabbin)	• Built candidate bank on Temp Desk
The Brotherhood of St. Laurence	• Case managed long-term unemployed • Ran 'Parents as Career Transition Support' PACTS training in local secondary colleges
YES – Your Employment Solutions (Frankston) • National Archives Australia (NAA)	• Case managed long-term unemployed • Supervised 'Work for the Dole' WftD project • Preserving immigration records for NAA
Top Jobs (Hastings/ Mornington) (State Gov. Project) **FMPLLEN**	• Assisted youth into apprenticeships/traineeships • Designed and ran programs to build employability skills • On panel to choose secondary students for awards
Career Advice Australia (Hastings) (C/wealth Gov. Project) • FMPLLEN • SkillsPlus • The Brotherhood of St. Laurence	• Worked with schools, agencies, local government and community supporting transition services to employment and further education • Assisted networks to provide career options to students • Participated in Career Program with HMAS Cerberus • Trained teachers to facilitate PACTS training • Worked with Careers Teachers to introduce programmes suited to their students' needs
SkillsPlus (Moorabbin)	• Risk assessed WftD projects • Sourced not-for-profits willing to offer WftD places • Mentored junior consultant

Paramount Personnel (Headhunted for role) (Frankston, Cranbourne & Pakenham)	• Assessed capacity of new job seekers with a disability • Conducted job search training • Oversaw 3 offices job search training • Wrote training packages for job search training/ basic computer skills • Assessed job roles and wrote procedures for clients
Link Employment & Training (Dandenong)	• Managed Technical Training Facility (Automotive and Building & Construction)
Max Employment (Chelsea)	• Managed Disability Services office
PENstep (Headhunted for role) (Mornington Peninsula) **Mornington Peninsula Shire**	• Assisted Mornington Peninsula small to medium-sized businesses to source applicants for hard to fill vacancies
Sarina Russo (Headhunted for role) (Frankston)	• Part of the tender team for proposed WftD Contract • Networking with contacts to gain support for tender
Disability Training Organisation	• Wrote training resources
Training Resource Centre – TRC (Headhunted for role)	• Proofread training resources

About the Author

Pauline Visser Employment Coaching	Wrote training package "Back on track and ready to go". **Small Business**: • screening candidates • reference checking • Policy/Procedures • Position Descriptions • customised assistance **Individuals:** • resume/applications • employment coaching

Introduction

"The only place where success comes before work is in the dictionary".
    Brian Tracy

This book is about the recruitment process and how to get it right. When you know how, you'll give yourself the best opportunity to either secure that right job, employ the best candidate or help somebody else find sustainable employment.

The information in *Eight Essential Elements to Employment*, draws on the experiences, skills, knowledge and wisdom not only of myself but of many other professionals I am grateful to have in my network.

Special thanks to the following who contributed to 'Experts in my network say':

    Jo Johnson, The Content Coach
    Debbie Flintoff-King, Gold Medal Olympian
    Angela Jacobsen, 'OzSuperNanny'

> Rodney Molloy, Owner, CanAussie Tech Ltd
>
> Mary Tresize-Brown, Development Officer- Schools & Community SE LLEN
>
> Gaye Kidder, Managing Director, LEC Recruitment
>
> Peta McIver, Senior IT Consultant, PAXUS (previously)
>
> Dave Thomas, Case Manager (previously)
>
> Linda Perrins, Correspondence/Complaints Clerk (previously)

Thanks to the following for their role in producing this book:

> Mentor/Coach/Editor/Expert – Jo Johnson, 'The Content Coach'
>
> Publisher – Blaise van Hecke, Busybird Publishing
>
> Foreword – Lyn Cairns, Director, Qudos Recruitment
>
> Photographer – Janis House, Janis House Photography
>
> Hair and Makeup (photo shoot) – Helen Clarke, HC Makeup & Hair
>
> For walking down the path with me, - my lovely daughters, Georgia & Christie Visser
>
> Illustrator/Artist – Ishika Rai, Year 11 Student
>
> Proofreader – Dianne Wadsworth, Gumhill Proofreading
>
> Logo design – Derek Warner, 'Warner Signs'
>
> Spontaneous editing and logo design – Georgia Visser

And a huge thanks to all of the individuals, business professionals, consultants, applicants, clients and jobseekers who provided testimonials or were the subjects of the real life stories.

Illustrator/Artist

Ishika Rai is a Year 11 student at John Paul College in Frankston on the Mornington Peninsula. She is a very promising artistic talent as you will see from her significant contributions to this book. I stumbled upon her artwork quite by accident one morning whilst ordering my usual *soy chai latte* at a local café, following a tiring shopping expedition that called for a pit stop prior to heading home.

The truth is, I don't believe this was an accident or a coincidence, because it has proven to be one of the most serendipitous moments of recent times. I am familiar with these sorts of moments as evidenced throughout my many years of family history research. In fact I discovered one of my ancestors was a Chinese interpreter in the heady gold rush days in Ballarat. But that is another story for another day.

Back to Ishika. Whilst waiting for my order I made mention to the barista that I liked the beautiful and distinctive decorations on the cups used to illustrate the different sizes of drinks available. My throw away comment was how the designs reminded me of *Ishka* (a shop that stocks beautiful brightly coloured homewares and clothes from places such as Morocco and India and which is a particular favourite of mine). The barista went on to explain that the drawings were done by one of the part-time staff who worked there; doodles completed in her quiet moments between customers to make the display cups more attractive.

I needed to learn more of this Ishika who *almost* shared a name with the delicious shop I adore (coincidence?), who drew amazing Middle Eastern-looking floral swirls on her own initiative as a way to avoid idle hands.

Skip forward a couple of weeks, and with some career aspiration conversations and a high degree of enthusiasm for my project, Ishika agreed to contribute her artistic talent to my book.

In her own words:

> "Art is not what you see, but what you make others see".
> Edgar Degas, Artist

Hi, I'm Ishika Rai, and am currently studying year 11 at John Paul College. Art comes in many different forms, each of which have been a part of my life for a very long time. I took a huge interest in painting and drawing about halfway through primary school and haven't put the paint brush down since.

When Pauline Visser approached me about illustrating her book, I was thrilled that I had been offered such an enriching opportunity. Having my artwork noticed and appreciated by the public is something that brings me a lot of joy, and this wouldn't have been possible without the display of my artwork at 'Espresso Bar' in Bayside where I currently work part-time. From winning competitions at school to having my art work displayed at Art Galleries, this opportunity allows me to further develop my passion for art. The most recent prize I won at school was for my painting 'Destination'. This is quite appropriate as the painting I have done for the cover of Pauline's book (*Eight Essential Elements to Employment*) is about being on the 'right path', both feature a person walking along a pathway.

Art is something that I have studied for many years, and this opportunity will only fuel my love for it more. Lastly, I'd like to congratulate and thank Pauline as I couldn't be more grateful for being invited to be a part of something that will certainly be a large and successful contribution to the business world.

SECTION 1. The Customers

The Individual

The Business Professional

The Consultant

The Individual

Meet 'Indie' the Individual

'Indie' is typically 40-60 years of age, currently working, or just recently left a job. She/he is unappreciated, not happy, not fulfilled and knows there is something else out there that would make work less of a chore and much more enjoyable.

'Indie' knows the job better than others who are higher in the food chain and completes the work with high competency but somehow isn't noticed. All too often someone else is right there poised to take the credit for 'Indie's' efforts. Familiar story?

It is said, "If you love what you do, you will never work a day in your life". That is something we all desire but not many of us actually achieve. Sometimes we are caught in a job that pays the bills but isn't fulfilling a deeper need. It requires a lot of effort to make the change and find something better – but it's worth it when you end up loving what you do.

The Eight Essential Elements to Employment clearly sets out the steps along the path to secure a job that doesn't just provide the financial incentives you require, but also allows you to go to work every day and love what you do.

Meet me

I love living on the Mornington Peninsula in Victoria and especially enjoy living near the many beaches that are a stone's throw away. Both sides of the Peninsula offer beautiful scenery, a variety of beaches, a myriad of wineries, gourmet artisan food producers, and plenty of lush bushland and rolling hills in-between.

Everyone knows everyone on the Peninsula and this has assisted my career, believing as I do to never close doors behind me. This has proven to be a successful ethos by which to live and my career continues to benefit from this strategy. On many occasions my network has opened doors for me as I am somewhat known by reputation, however this hasn't happened by accident. I have purposely taken on roles that allow for the extension of existing skills with an element of new content to challenge me. In this way I am privy to a lifelong learning experience.

The truth is though, that my professional life has not always provided me with what I needed. I have worked hard to be successful at what I do but my ideas haven't always taken hold in the 'boys club' or, alternatively, the powerful female dominated environments that I have been drawn to. Over the years I have longed for a brighter future at work with a team that respected where I came from and what I had to offer. Above all I wanted to get that buzz that comes from being recognised for your capabilities and depth of knowledge – for being the 'go-to' person.

I wanted to show my children by example how NOT to work in a job that offers no joy or fulfilment. What would I be teaching my children about 'making-do' and putting up with less than rightful happiness if I was to work in a job I hated? Our work is such a big piece of who we are, our identity, and goodness knows we spend a lot of time doing it, so I didn't want to leave a legacy of drudgery and mediocrity.

My health and family relationships were too valuable for me to continue on the path I was on. So I finally took the leap, designed a business that suits my needs and gives me a way to work on my terms whilst still making a positive impact on others.

SECTION 1. The Customers

For the individual

You may be someone who is dissatisfied with your current role and know you are on the wrong path, or you may be unemployed seeking a suitable position. Regardless, you need to understand how to give yourself the best opportunity of reaching your goal. The *'Insider Insights'* contained in each chapter are particularly relevant to you. These are my top tips, which can quickly improve your chances of success.

Additionally, the *'What the experts in my network say'* section provides you with a broad range of valuable expertise and points of view from other professionals. I have pulled together information from some amazing people whom I have had the benefit of working with – or for – in many different organisations. You won't find access to this wealth of knowledge all in one place, anywhere else.

▣ Tables of resources for 'Indie' the Individual

> **Table i) The Recruitment Process** table clearly outlines the order of steps undertaken in a full recruitment process. This table is a visual representation of the *Eight Essential Elements to Employment,* with a focus on actions and tasks.
>
> **Table ii) Adjectives for a Rocking Resume** is a guide to help you better describe the duties you have performed in jobs that will make your resume more interesting and professional.

▣ Resources for 'Indie' the Individual

> **Table i) The Recruitment Process** Following these steps will help you to approach recruitment in a chronological manner getting the most from your efforts and giving you the best chance at success. Working through this structure as well as using the individual chapters with their easy-to-digest tables, will give you the essential components to recruitment success.

Action	Task	Location
'Motivate yourself'	"Get your mind in the right place … "	Chapter 1 See Blog
'Present yourself'	"Making a good first impression … "	Chapter 2 See Blog
'Upskill yourself' decide	"Are you prepared for change?" • on interests • on industry/field • on position to apply for	Chapter 3 See Blog
'Amazing Application' search research prepare apply	"What is the purpose of the Application?" • for position • business/company/organisation • application • for position	Chapter 4 See Blog
'Rocking Resume' prepare apply record	"What is the purpose of the Resume?" • resume • for position • your applications	Chapter 5 See Blog
'Pre-interview' prepare/research	"Ready, set, go! When does the interview actually begin?" • before the interview	Chapter 6 See Blog
'In interview' follow preparation	"Avoid desperation, relax and be you" • during the interview	Chapter 7 See Blog
'Post-interview' follow-up negotiate/accept/reject retain	"Thoughts to digest" • after the interview • an offer • the position	Chapter 8 See Blog

SECTION 1. The Customers

Resources for 'Indie' the Individual continued:

Table ii) Adjectives for Rocking Resume using the consistent suffix '-ing' makes the flow of information easier to absorb with a less jarring effect. Use this individual approach at resume compilation as a point of difference to candidates who use bulk templates. Can you add to the list? (This is not necessarily an all-inclusive listing).

• accessing	• mapping
• achieving	• marketing
• administering	• meeting
• analysing	• negotiating
• appraising	• networking
• assessing	• observing
• assisting	• obtaining
• arranging	• organising
• balancing	• participating
• building	• preparing
• checking	• pre-screening
• compiling	• presenting
• completing	• processing
• complying	• producing
• conducting	• providing
• consulting	• recording
• continuing	• referring
• counselling	• reporting
• designing	• researching
• developing	• reviewing
• drafting	• rewriting
• driving	• rostering
• engaging	• running
• ensuring	• scheduling
• expanding	• setting
• identifying	• supervising
• initiating	• taking
• interpreting	• testing
• leading	• updating
• liaising	• working

• maintaining	• writing
• managing	

Stories

The day I was approached by *Brad* at the Sandbelt Hotel (it's not what you are thinking!), came as a big surprise to me. His group of work colleagues (who were all grinning as they watched him approach me at the bar) had deputised him to settle their argument. As I focussed on the people sitting around the distant table, it slowly dawned on me who they were. The faces in the dim light gradually grew clearer and I realised that they were previous recruits of mine – from some twenty years earlier! They all wanted to thank me for choosing *them* all of those years ago. Why? Because that decision had set each of them on a career path that had completely transformed their lives. Many of them had subsequently been promoted many times, worked overseas and offered opportunities that they had not imagined possible back then.
This is the true story of Brad and a table of grateful recruits

Neil was recruited to a key middle management role that required regular domestic travel with a team of buyers. It was vital for any new team member to fit in quickly and seamlessly. Subsequently, the screening process for candidates included a dinner with the team to ensure their social etiquette was in line with the business culture. The role required dining frequently with suppliers, and it was imperative that the manager and the team represented the organisation appropriately. After a lengthy and gruelling shortlisting and selection process, *Neil* was chosen. To my surprise, I ran into *Neil* again about twenty-five years later. By this time he was on the Board of Directors for an organisation whose management team I had recently joined. We met at an awards night and he was quick to acknowledge that one of the key reasons that he was actually on that Board was the path travelled as a result of the buyer role appointment, many years earlier.
This is the true story of Neil (recruit)

SECTION 1. *The Customers*

Testimonials

"Objective and very professional advice – maximising impact of resume. Thank you".
    Gerardine (Client)

"Pauline was very thorough and efficient when preparing my resume. My updated resume was then a professional, effective document".
    Tess (Job seeker)

"The resume and cover letter were perfectly suited to the position I was applying for with keywords highlighted from the ad".
    Jacqui (Client)

"My working relationship with Pauline dates back to the early 1990's when she was the Personnel Officer of a major American corporate and I was an IT specialist recruiter sourcing permanent and contract staff for their IT consulting division. I recall enjoying an excellent relationship with Pauline. She was always supportive, responsive, professional and together we were able to satisfy some lofty expectations in a challenging environment".
    Peta McIver (Consultant with preferred supplier)

The Business Professional

Meet 'Al' the Business Professional
The over-stretched business professional, 'Al', is already putting in long days just to keep up with the latest management priority. 'Al' has plenty of technical skills and experience to perform the tasks required in the business, but is often placed under direct pressure to step outside of existing priorities. When one of 'Al's' staff resigns, everyone groans, because it means the workload will increase considerably until he can be replaced. An unplanned, and therefore not prioritised recruitment, temporarily overrides the other demands that already exist. It means lengthy working hours and heightened pressure for 'Al' and his team until the vacancy is filled.

Meet me
I have worked for many private recruitment agencies in both generalist and specialist roles (accounting, clerical, manufacturing). When working on a temporary assignment I was encouraged to apply for an internal vacancy as a Personnel Officer. It took some convincing, as I felt ill-equipped for the enormous role working for a major

manufacturer with some 800 employees. Two interviews, a medical and battery of psychological tests later, and the job was mine.

Many travel opportunities were afforded me in that role as I had to recruit staff in Sydney, Adelaide and Darwin. There were also other projects to manage: designing the testing regime required to open a new facility in Malaysia; and conducting research to assist with plans to move production into Eastern Europe. A training programme was then designed and implemented by my manager and myself for about 70 line managers, teaching them how to better participate in the recruitment of their staff.

So as you can see, I have been in the same situation as you. The role I held with the largest multinational food manufacturer at the time was fast moving, dynamic, demanding and all encompassing. My specific experience recruiting staff to complement a multitude of different teams makes me a valuable resource for you as a hiring manager.

If you find yourself in 'Al's' position, you need to ask: "Am I on the right path to quickly and successfully securing a new team member"? If the answer is no, if you are feeling overwhelmed, then the information in this book will be sure to help.

For the Business Professional

As a team leader or manager, you no doubt have incredible expertise in your field. You will most certainly also have excellent leadership skills. However, not always do great leaders or technicians have the skills required to effectively recruit people. Thankfully there is help available to make this process efficient and effective.

Time management is an essential component of running an effective team. However, when you're down on headcount you're also down on productivity. So, any help you can get to fill that gap quickly, with the right person, will allow you to focus on your core business priorities. The 'Tables of resources' provides information about the recruitment process that will assist you in filling your vacancies in a timely manner.

The 'Insider Insights' section of each chapter is a collection of tips that took me 30 years to gather. Sharing those insights with you, along with the resources provided, is my pleasure. Your success is my success!

- **Tables of resources for 'Al' the Business Professional:**

> **Table iii) The Recruitment Process** provides information regarding the order and essential elements in the process to employment. This is particularly useful as it details when to raise a document and the reasons for doing so. It will help to keep your Human Resources records in a structured manner and ensure you are well prepared for future reviews, requests, audits etc.
>
> **Table iv) Scoring candidates in interview** provides a template for use when interviewing to ensure you are making like-with-like comparisons. The document will assist you with making a selection based on the position description and will become a record that clearly outlines the logic behind staff appointments. Whilst there are some useful assumptions made about a candidate's first impression at interview, by using a template that is relevant to the selection criteria you end up with a more considered and objective grading system. Your final selection will no doubt reflect both the scores and the overall impression you were left with but the structured score sheet helps compare apples with apples and is useful to have on file as a record of why each appointment was made.

SECTION 1. The Customers

🗎 Resources for 'Al' the Business Professional

Table iii) The Recruitment Process is a type of flow chart that identifies the various steps in the process. This process commences when you receive a resignation, somebody is terminated or you require an additional team member for growth. Use the table key to prompt you to create a file, raise a document, compose advertising or send correspondence.

Task	Action	Result
APPROVAL		
seek approval	to begin recruiting	YES V / NO >
review existing team	to promote /demote, change/merge roles	YES V / NO >
review needs of the business	to determine changes in demand/supply, trends in business/budgetary constraints	YES V / NO >
discuss findings with manager	to justify the decision to recruit	YES V / NO >
gain written approval	to create a paper trail (as required)	YES V / NO >
record commencement of recruitment	to report against budget (as required)	
N.B. *The order of these actions may vary from organisation to organisation.*		**Table iii) Key:** 🗎 Document 📁 File 📰 Advertising ✉ Letter
	PREPARATION	

13

conduct research	access 'Recruitment Policies and Procedures'	follow procedures
prepare	• recruitment schedule, working backwards from proposed start date to determine commencement of recruitment date • recruitment file, adhering to procedures to ensure all reporting policies are followed	**Document:** 📄 Recruitment Schedule 📁 Recruitment File
prepare	• recruitment strategy, including: advertising medium, candidate search process (internal, external, networking, agency), a list of interviewers, process for subsequent interviews and any testing required	**Document:** 📄 Recruitment Strategy
review and update	position description	**Document:** 📄 Position Description (updated)
gain approval and/or negotiate	to amend salary (if required)	YES ✓ /NO >
record	salary level and package entitlements	update 📁 Recruitment File
	CANDIDATE SEARCH	
access	Resumes already on file from previous recruitment campaigns	place in 📁 Recruitment File
create and place	advertising copy, including any media or company branding stipulations	**Document:** 📰 Advertising copy
contact	Recruitment agencies and brief them on your requirements including team culture and fit	

provide	Recruitment Agency	📄 Position description
plan and implement	Networking strategy. This may include headhunting, asking staff for recommendations or accessing your own professional network.	

	INTERVIEW PREPARATION	
prepare	• interview questions and format • interview schedule	see 'Recruitment Procedures' of your organisation **Document:** 📄 Interview Questions 📄 Interview Schedule
schedule	place interview times in diary: • book venue • advise administration staff • select and advise other suitable interview participants	
provide	interview questions and schedule to fellow interviewers	
Receive	recruitment agency candidates	update 📁 Recruitment File

SECTION 1. The Customers

	RECEIVE APPLICATIONS	
accept and acknowledge record	Applications with the appropriate Standard Letter applications	**Document:** ✉ Standard Letter (appropriate to the source of the candidate) update 📁 Recruitment File
shortlist	applications	update 📁 Recruitment File
	INTERVIEW	
invite	shortlisted applicants to attend interview	update 📁 Recruitment File
prepare	venue for interviews by: • ensuring adequate seating is arranged, water is provided, phone is on silent and sign is on the door • provide reception staff with interview schedule • brief other interviewers on interview format (to ensure consistent goals)	
conduct	interviews referring to: • interview schedule • interview questions • recruitment schedule • recruitment file detailing salary and package entitlements	**Document:** 📄 Interview Questions

gather	reference checking information (of at least three suitable referees) from all interviewed candidates	
discuss	with fellow interviewers: • results of interview • answers to interview questions • scores (that have been individually tallied and recorded first)	update 🗁 Recruitment File
agree	on a shortlist	update 🗁 Recruitment File
(If appropriate) arrange review update	second interviews results from 2nd interview recruitment file	

	REVIEWING	
score	Candidates	
conduct	reference checks, medicals and any other testing required	
select	successful candidate	update 📁 Recruitment File
	OFFER	
verbally offer position	to preferred candidate, and negotiate package and start date and any probation period if appropriate	
prepare	Contract	**Document:** ✉ Letter of Offer
plan and advise	induction program ensuring all appropriate people are notified	**Document:** 📄 Induction Schedule
announce	commencement of new employee to existing staff/board	
advise	pay office of commencement	**Document:** 📄 Admission to Payroll (as required)

Resources for 'Al' the Business Professional continued:

Table iv) Scoring candidates in interview is done to make direct comparisons based on answers to a standard list of questions. These questions should be drawn directly from the Selection Criteria detailed in the Position Description. These should, by definition, also be the key things you are seeking in the successful candidate. The following table should cover all items on the selection criteria; of course it can be adapted as required. Request specific examples from the candidate for each question; this not only shows suitable experience and preparation but the ability to think on their feet.

Example question	Reference to PD	Comments	Score
What is the most successful team you have been part of? (including examples of the success)	Criteria 1.		/5
When were you most challenged in a job and what strategies did you use to overcome the challenges?	Criteria 2.		/5
What was your greatest achievement in your current job and how was it measured by your manager?	Criteria 3.		/5
Do you prefer to lead your team or participate as a team member? When have you done both?	Criteria 4.		/5
How have you used your initiative in the workplace and how was it received?	Criteria 5.		/5
Total score			/25

SECTION 1. The Customers

Beware the human factor! Even if you are 100% prepared and certain about your recruitment process you cannot predict what might happen. Human beings are not robots. Some of the best recruitment matches on paper have fallen apart because something unforeseen happened. Generally speaking however, past behaviour is a good predictor of future behaviour and this is largely what you rely on when selecting somebody to add to your team.

How do you know what you are being told is the truth? Use reference checking to ensure the information provided is accurate.

Top tips for effective reference checking:

- only talk to the most suitable referees
- read between the lines
- use conversation style (establish rapport) to gain the most honest information
- take notice of what isn't being said and pursue that line of questioning
- confirm duties and salary level
- always finish with "would you re-hire this person?"

At any point in the hiring journey, your preferred candidate may have a change in personal circumstances, which alters the desired outcome. However, by following my Recruitment Process, you give yourself the best possible chance at recruiting successfully.

Testimonials

"I felt it important to at least make comment to you of my admiration for the effort and conscientious diligence of Pauline Visser during the extensive Recruitment Program conducted during the first three months of this year. As you will not doubt be aware, a significant number of applicants were dealt with by Pauline and to a lesser part by myself. At all times during this recruitment program, Pauline showed dedication and her enthusiasm made it a pleasure to work with her. With such a large number of applicants and vacancies to fill in a somewhat constrained period the results show that in Pauline we have an employee with a valuable sense of duty. I would like to say ... what a fine job she does".

>Richard (Department Manager) Philip Morris Ltd. (written to Human Resources Manager)

"In running a busy Labour Hire and Recruitment firm I often find I am short on talent or relevant candidates to fill our many vacancies. Utilising Pauline's expertise to help manage our overflow, I found her service to be sharp, concise and thorough. Her well-written candidate profiles and alternate candidate sourcing methods have enabled Skillinvest to save and retain key clients keeping us ahead of our competitors".

>Paul Konig, Acting General Manager
>Metro, Skillinvest

"Pauline and I worked together for a number of years in community learning and development. She has a wealth of skills and knowledge in employment and training as well as great organisational skills so sharing all of these in a book will be an excellent resource for us all".
    Mary Tresize-Brown, Development Officer
    – Schools & Community SE LLEN

The Consultant

Meet 'Con' the Consultant
Working hard in a busy Jobactive Office or a Recruitment Agency, there are many demands on 'Con's' time and it takes a lot of discipline and effort to keep up with the highly demanding, process-driven environment. There are competing priorities for 'Con' in the Jobactive Office, with both employer and candidates vying for his attention. 'Con' is there because he wants to assist people into employment, but it feels more like he spends too much time navigating the electronic calendar of appointments that can be double or triple booked – mostly by someone else.

For 'Con' at the Private Recruitment Agency the days are long and highly pressured; there are both clients and candidates demanding attention, and sales targets to meet. There is also business development for new clients to be done and regular reporting to be completed.

Meet me
For me, it is all about respect for my clients and candidates. I

possess a genuine desire to improve people's futures by matching them with a suitable, sustainable role that will change their paths; I have never been interested in filling a spot to make the sale so I could move on to the next. Being the catalyst for life-changing improvement lights me up. Witnessing the changes that happen in people's lives when they work at something they truly love is a huge reward.

I know this approach works because I have seen the results over and over again!

From the very first time I worked in the employment industry I knew it was demanding and challenging, but it made me feel alive. Dealing with confidential sensitivities and helping others to change their lives for the better is very rewarding.

Every time a candidate wanted to give up on finding a job because they had tried so hard and got nowhere, my reply was always: "if you stop now, you won't find out if the next application is the successful one". I encouraged them by saying: "keep going and don't give up ... I believe in you ... it's a numbers game ... the next job you apply for could be the one ... you only want one job".

With a copy of *Eight Essential Elements to Employment* as a reference document you will be offering your own version of positive motivation within no time. Your early days in the recruitment industry will be significantly easier to navigate by having this resource to refer to and gain inspiration from.

How do I know this? I have been in your place, working for many private recruitment companies, job network providers and in private industry in a large multinational manufacturer during the course of my career. Tapping in to the knowledge I have will increase your chances of success in this industry.

For the Consultant

You may be a consultant working in the employment industry who is new to the role or just seeking to increase your skills. Your job may be in the Commonwealth Government's Jobactive (previously known as Job Network) or a private personnel agency. As a new consultant you will have much to learn quickly in a fast moving environment. There are protocols, confidentiality legalities, contract requirements, employment laws, business norms (for your particular organisation), processes, procedures, policies and much, much more. The sections titled *'What the experts in my network say'* and *'References'* that are included in each chapter, will be very useful to you as they provide top tips from others who have already walked the path you are on. More experienced consultants will equally find this resource of lists, processes and other source material, to be of enormous benefit.

As an Employment Consultant you have to remember that there is a job for everyone and your job is to provide the motivation, skills and resources to find it. Even though candidates may place the emphasis on you getting them a job, in reality it is up to them to put in the work to achieve that result – you are there as a guide and conduit.

You will be faced with clients who have little or no work history. Uncovering transferrable skills will be very useful when compiling resumes. Many clients will not know what type of work they actually want and will be looking for your guidance. (See Chapter 3, 'Upskill yourself')

I have found *'The Job Guide'* an extremely useful resource and have used it in the following ways:

- identifying occupations of interest
- understanding what duties are performed in jobs
- learning which jobs have little need
- identifying similar jobs
- knowing what personal qualities are useful in different jobs
- working out jobs that may be suitable because you were good at science for example
- skill shortages
- charts of occupations by classification e.g. scientific

If you haven't discovered this yet, you should spend some time exploring the many ways this one resource can assist you in your job. The value of it being updated each year ensures you have access to the latest information available to the government. (Available in hard copy at newsagencies and online.)

My intention for *Eight Essential Elements to Employment* is that it also becomes a valuable resource for you and that you think of it as your Consultant's Handbook.

Respect and empathy

Working with empathy means "having to walk a mile in the apache's shoes", and you are going to need empathy in bucket loads to be a great consultant. When you remember that we all have different backgrounds, experiences and different coping mechanisms, you will be more able to help people effectively. The clients you work with will have often seen many consultants previously and may by now be quite disillusioned. Finding work is a hard road for many, but as our jobs are often at the core of our self-esteem and identity, it's essential to treat everybody with respect. Using respect as the starting point with every client is a solid beginning. It allows you to develop a working relationship of mutual regard, remembering that everyone has his or her own story. Prejudices and judgements need to be left outside the room when you are conducting your client appointments.

Maslow's hierarchy of needs (See Table of Definitions)

When working with clients remember that their basic physiological needs (food, water, warmth, shelter) have to be met before they will be able to focus on seeking employment. This is why it is important to develop a good rapport with new clients so they are comfortable enough to open up and truthfully discuss their current situation. Once you understand what issues they are facing you are much better equipped to offer the appropriate level of assistance. Sometimes working with Jobactive clients means supporting them to take small steps in the right direction. Over time a lot of small steps add up to the change required to find and retain sustainable employment. Many jobseekers that have been unemployed long term become quite jaded with the 'system' and can find telling their story all over again to *another* Consultant very challenging. The time you spend building rapport with your clients and understanding their barriers will ultimately become the key to your success.

Workload

Speaking from experience, I am well aware that a consultant's workload is usually extremely high, which means not a lot of time to spend with each individual client. It's therefore vital to use the regular time you *do* have as wisely as possible, by identifying the key area that is preventing them from securing a job. There may well be more than one barrier to work on however, so be sure to tackle the most important things that will have the biggest impact. Don't let your client distract you with excuses, reasons or negativity, but instead focus on the best way to help improve their life in the most efficient way possible. It is a balance between meeting the requirements of your employer and addressing the needs of your clients. When time is your enemy make sure you use it effectively!

Footnote on your safety

Your safety and security should be high on the list of priorities of the way you perform your job. Having worked for a large number of the Job Network Agencies, I am aware that sometimes your safety can be compromised. You may find yourself placed in difficult situations so be aware and do everything you can to ensure your wellbeing.

Stories

The Saga of Ella
When working for a Disability Provider and rostered on alone, I discovered just how important safety and security are. Ella was late for her appointment. Relief was beginning to wash over my body as I considered all the tasks I could get done in the next

20 unscheduled minutes. Then I heard it, the strange dragging sound coming from the long corridor outside the office door. I sat perfectly still listening while I tried to recognise the noise or the reason for it. It was like no sound I had heard before. Before I had time to think, the office door was flung open and Ella spilled in and collapsed onto the floor. I realised then that that was what the noise was – Ella had been dragging herself along the tiles towards me, in the hope of finding assistance.

So now I was alone with a client unconscious on the floor – a situation I was definitely not prepared for. Was she dead? What would I do with her? Could I leave her there and get help? It was up to me alone to find out!

Fast forward to the final chapter of this saga, she wasn't dead, just unconscious and very unwell. Thankfully the ambulance arrived in time to take Ella to the hospital where she recovered. I was shaken for a while, but just happy that I was able to assist Ella.

The moral of the story is that you need to expect the unexpected and be ready to make good decisions if you are placed in a difficult position. My situation could have ended very differently.

No consultant should be left alone, particularly if dealing with clients who are drug addicted or suffering from mental illness.

Full moon

Whether the next story has scientific grounds on which to rest, I do not know. However I can give you multiple anecdotal tales of the woe of how the full moon affects clients of Jobactive and Disability Services.

Raised voices coming from reception raised alarm bells for everyone. The unspoken procedure was that the consultants would circle around the office like sharks going in for the kill or like lions protecting their young from imminent threat. Good training in how to deal with difficult clients came in handy in these situations. By allowing the disgruntled client to talk out their frustrations we could quickly establish the reason for the dissatisfaction and then address it. Offering an empathetic ear, rather than a combative tone, meant these situations were often diffused as quickly as they began.

Nine times out of ten, having escorted the client from the office after one of these situations, we would all look at each other and realise that yes, it was indeed a full moon day.

- Resources for 'Con' the Consultant:

> **Table i) The Recruitment Process** is information regarding the order of recruitment. This table details the process described within the book in a visual way that focuses on actions and tasks.
> **Table ii) Adjectives for a Rocking Resume** is a guide to get you thinking about ways to describe duties that clients have performed in jobs, when compiling a resume. This will make their resume professional and interesting for the reader.

- Resources for 'Con' the Consultant:

> **Table i) The Recruitment Process** Following these steps will help your clients to approach recruitment in a chronological manner, getting the most from their efforts and giving them the best chance at success. You can walk them through this structure and also use the information in the individual chapters to help them understand the essential components to recruitment success.

Action	Task	Location
'Motivate yourself'	"Get your mind in the right place …"	Chapter 1 See Blog
'Present yourself'	"Make a good first impression …"	Chapter 2 See Blog

SECTION 1. The Customers

'Upskill yourself' decide	"Are you prepared for change?" • on interests • on industry/field • on position to apply for	Chapter 3 See Blog
'Amazing Application' research prepare/apply	"What is the purpose of the Application?" business/company/organisation for position	Chapter 4 See Blog
'Rocking Resume' prepare apply record	"What is the purpose of the Resume?" your application for position your application	Chapter 5 See Blog
'Pre-interview' prepare/research	"Ready, set, go! When does the interview actually begin?" before the interview	Chapter 6 See Blog
'In Interview' follow through	"Avoid desperation, relax and be you" during the interview	Chapter 7 See Blog
'Post-interview' follow-up negotiate/accept/reject retain	"Thoughts to digest" after the interview an offer the position	Chapter 8 See Blog

📄 Resources for 'Con' the Consultant continued:

> **Table ii) Adjectives for a Rocking Resume** Using the consistent suffix 'ing' makes the flow of information easier to consume, creating a less jarring effect for the reader. Use this approach when preparing a resume for your clients, as a point of difference from those who use bulk templates.
> Can you add to the list? (There are more to add to the list).

• accessing	• mapping
• achieving	• marketing
• administering	• meeting
• analysing	• negotiating
• appraising	• networking
• assessing	• observing
• assisting	• obtaining
• arranging	• organising
• balancing	• participating
• building	• preparing
• checking	• pre-screening
• compiling	• presenting
• completing	• processing
• complying	• producing
• conducting	• providing
• consulting	• recording
• continuing	• referring
• counselling	• reporting
• designing	• researching
• developing	• reviewing
• drafting	• rewriting
• driving	• rostering

• engaging	• running
• ensuring	• scheduling
• expanding	• setting
• identifying	• supervising
• initiating	• taking
• interpreting	• testing
• leading	• updating
• liaising	• working
• maintaining	• writing
• managing	

Story

When *Kevin* arrived for his 'compulsory' fortnightly appointments, with his tattered blue folder under one arm, it was bulging with records of his applications. There were literally hundreds of them that had been carefully filed inside. With a mixture of pride (for his persistence) and disappointment (that his efforts had not yet achieved the desired outcome) he would again walk me through his activity and the effort he had invested. After another arduous fortnight of effort with nothing to show for it, except more rejection letters, he was quiet, lacking motivation and despondent. I continued our now long-established ritual of picking him back up and re-launching him into the world re-motivated for the next fortnight.

We would go through the large number of jobs he had applied for in the preceding fortnight and fine tune the targeting to ensure he was applying for the most suitable roles. Keeping him on track to locate and successfully apply for suitable jobs was my main objective. However, his waning motivation understandably became a priority to address, as with each unsuccessful application the stamina and drive drained from his body.

Then one day, as predicted, he *did* find the job for him.

The day he walked into the office beaming and hurled that blue folder onto my desk, he knew it was for the last time. That folder represented a huge chunk of his life, a particularly difficult time that he was ecstatic to put behind him. He had done it: secured a job, a great job that he went on to hold for the remainder of his working life.

It was with a sense of sheer relief that his journey towards employment was over. His exhilaration was palpable and as a regular client for at least a year, the whole office celebrated his triumph. He had finally done it! He not only changed his life by discovering the right path but created positive and far reaching ripples throughout his family, allowing a release from the burden he had been carrying for so long. We talked about the job with 'his name on it' for so many months and now it was real.

The reference he wrote acknowledging the support and advice I gave him during this time is a valuable memento that I still retain some fifteen years on.

> "I will really miss your efforts to give me the courage to continue to keep applying for jobs, week after week, even when things looked hopeless".
> Kevin (Job seeker)

> "I have always found you to be very supportive and helpful in my endeavours to find work".
> Kevin (Job seeker)

SECTION 1. The Customers

Testimonials

"Pauline Visser was my Case Manager and has been a great help for me in finding a position".
    Frances (Job seeker)

"This is to let you know that with my age and inexperience it was very near impossible for me to get a job, but with Pauline Visser's help and experience with my resume, courses and searching for the right job, I found the perfect position that will happily last me for the rest of my working life".
    Reg (Job seeker)

SECTION 2. The Elements

The Eight Essential Elements to Employment

Flowchart

The Eight Essential Elements to Employment

What are the eight elements and why are they all essential?

If you are not having success when trying to get that job, consider this: are you following all eight essential steps to reach your goal?

Lots of people are great at some or many of the steps but fall short in a particular area that ultimately prevents them from reaching the desired outcome. You may have the best resume in the world, but if your personal presentation (for example), isn't complementing it, then you have broken the chain. Successfully applying for a job is a *process* and if you see it as such, you will greatly increase your chances of success.

The eight chapters in this book take you through the pitfalls associated with finding, navigating, securing and retaining the right job for you. Stop relying on luck and trust in the process as it has proven to be successful over and over again. It is not arduous or complicated, but each step should be followed to give yourself the best chance at a positive result.

Chart a) Flowchart of The Eight Essential Elements to Employment

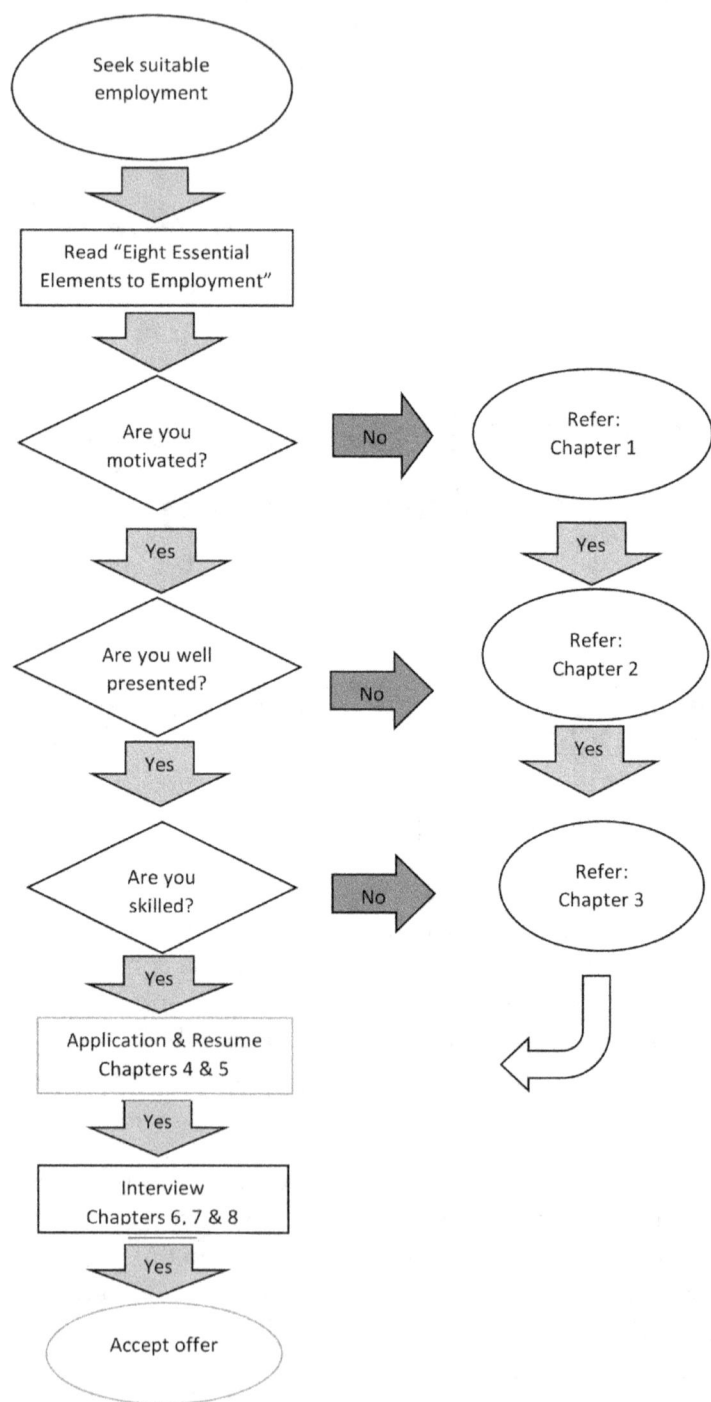

SECTION 3. The Chapters

Chapter 1: Motivate yourself

Chapter 2: Present yourself

Chapter 3: Upskill yourself

Chapter 4: Amazing Application

Chapter 5: Rocking Resume

Chapter 6: Pre-interview

Chapter 7: In Interview

Chapter 8: Post-interview

Structure of each chapter

Quotes:
🗨 Inspirational quotes relative to the material covered in the chapter

By the end of this chapter you will have a better understanding of:
✓ A summary of the learnings contained in the chapter

Blog:
💻 A body of information that stands alone on a topic and can be read as such. You may see this reproduced either in part or full in other forums. (E.g. website, social media, publications etc.)

Tables of resources:
📄 Tables that provide more specific information

Exercises:
✏ Interactive opportunity to practise the learning

Insider insights:
👆 Gleamed from a career in HR (Training, Recruitment and Employment). My personal job search/career progression experiences are also included.

- Some insights seem very obvious but often the obvious is overlooked.

Pitfalls/Rejection points:
- As you will see, there are many points throughout the recruitment process at which you can be eliminated and sent a dreaded rejection letter. You will be made aware of these trigger points and how to avoid them. Learning how to smooth out those bumps in your path to employment success, is what makes you much more likely to sit at the top of the shortlist.
- You might find yourself wondering if some of my stories or the points I make are a bit far-fetched, but I can assure you they are taken from real life examples – some so amazing you simply couldn't make them up! This firsthand knowledge of why people are screened out during the recruitment process is highly valuable knowledge that I want you to learn from.

Real life pitfall in action:
- True stories that illustrate pitfalls.

Experts in my network say:
- Pearls of wisdom from various people who have built their career, learned from their experiences and now possess knowledge that will benefit you.

Take a quick check-up:
- A list of soul searching questions designed to get you thinking about your current situation and how to improve it for success.

References:
- Further reading for those wishing to delve deeper into a particular topic.
- Online resources/apps

1
MOTIVATE YOURSELF

- "The way to get started is to quit talking and begin doing". *Disney*
- "The journey of a thousand miles begins with one step". *Lao Tzu*
- "Never give up! You can do anything you want by simply not giving up". *Turia Pitt*

By the end of this chapter you will have a better understanding of:
- ✓ how your attitude will make a difference to the outcome
- ✓ the power of positivity
- ✓ the value of motivation
- ✓ why to ditch desperation
- ✓ how to turn your negatives into positives

💻 Blog:

Is your head in the right space to convince the universe that you are the *best* candidate for the job? Start with your *powerhouse*, use your mind, and motivate yourself!

By doing so, you will be taking your first step onto the path that will lead you to greater fulfilment in your working life.

If you don't believe in yourself, and act like you don't believe in yourself, then you will have trouble convincing a stranger to believe in you in a 30 minute interview. So, start by motivating yourself!

If you *expect* success you won't take rejection and knockbacks personally; you will understand it is just part of the process. Missing out on a job gives you the chance to be better prepared for the next one. View it as a dress rehearsal for the right job for you. It is one step closer to success.

If you believe in the way the universe works, you could think, "it wasn't meant to be" or "if something is worth having, its worth working for". Sure they are old adages but never the less, commonly believed ones.

Try not to fall into the "woe is me" trap. Sometimes referred to in

SECTION 3. The Chapters

American self-help books as *"stinkin' thinkin'"* – this is to be avoided at all costs!

Turn your thinking around and notice the difference it makes.

Ways to get your thinking right:
- expecting failure is not an option, *expect success*
- believe that you are worthy and deserving
- be the *authentic* you
- practice *positive thinking*
- limit/eliminate negative influences
- know who or what robs your time/energy and shut it down
- take control of your moods
- turn "lemons into lemonade"
- mix with positive people
- spend time with people who have what you aim for
- believe in yourself
- know you can achieve what you desire
- "fake it until you make it"
- visualise how it will look and feel to achieve your goals
- expect a miracle
- compile a vision board

* Seek appropriate professional assistance if you feel an inability to manage this without support.

Table of resources for Chapter 1:

> **Table v) Goal setting** is important if you want to arrive at the correct destination, otherwise why use a GPS in a car or a map to find treasure?

▤ **Table of resources for Chapter 1:**

> **Table v) Goal setting** is a valuable and worthwhile thing to do. It is often said that if you don't know which road to travel you will not arrive at your desired destination. Setting goals is a good way to map out and work towards a better future.
> When setting goals, make sure they are motivating, then write them down, commit to them and stick with them.
> Goals should be **SMART: S**pecific, **M**easurable, **A**ttainable, **R**elevant and Time Bound.

Item	Objective	Time frame
	SHORT TERM	
Apply for jobs	Be happy at work	For 4 weeks
Prepare for success	Be happy at work	For 4 weeks
Measure progress of applications	To determine why it is not working	For 4 weeks
Adjust methods	To increase chances of success	At end of 4 weeks
		In 2 months
		In 2 months
		In 2 months

	LONG TERM	
Improve overall happiness	Enjoy work	3 months
Work in a great team	Feel included and appreciated	3 months
Be rewarded for my efforts	Have job satisfaction	3 months
Can see a career path ahead	Promotion	3 months
Increase income	Promotion	3 – 6 months
		1 year
		1 year
		5 years
		5 years

Exercise/s:
✎ Continue filling out Table v) 'Goal setting' using the SMART formula.

Insider insights:
- 👍 Treat this process seriously and you are more likely to get a serious outcome.
- 👍 Take a holistic approach and remember, your attitude reflects how you feel.
- 👍 Consider your life balance, diet, exercise, relationships, etc. and do what you can to be in the right headspace when you are approaching a job/career change.
- 👍 Undertake activities to keep your mind focused and positive – meditate, spend time alone, walk on the beach, listen to music, talk to someone close to you, pat your pet.
- 👍 Never burn your bridges.
- 👍 above all, eliminate desperation, as it oozes out of your pores and can be smelt a mile away by a recruiter

Pitfalls/Rejection points:
- Desperation should be avoided as it can lead to making poor choices.
- Negative attitudes can lead others to believe this is your usual demeanour.
- Your attitude at interview, when you are trying to impress, is expected to be the best it will ever be.
- Reacting badly to rejection or delays can burn your bridges for the future.
- Being argumentative or disagreeable with the interviewer.

Real life pitfall in action:
It wasn't obvious that Mr Jagged Rocks was a loose cannon until the results of the Psychological Testing arrived with the strong recommendation NOT to proceed with this candidate. Taking on board the professional advice that had been sought, the candidate was subsequently rejected. Suddenly the water was pulled out by the tide and the jagged rocks appeared from below the surface in a tirade of insults. My call to advise the candidate he was not successful turned nasty very quickly, confirming for me that the advice that had been given was correct. That was a close call!

Experts in my network say:

➤ "Only the pain of a hard workout will save the agony of defeat".   Debbie Flintoff-King, Gold Medallist, Seoul Olympics 1988

➤ "It's not what annoys you that matters, it's how you react to it that counts".
    Debbie Flintoff-King,
      Gold Medallist, Seoul Olympics 1988

SECTION 3. The Chapters

> ➤ "Whether you think you can or whether you think you can't, you will be right".
>
> *Debbie Flintoff-King,*
>   Gold Medallist, Seoul Olympics 1988

> ➤ "Don't give up, especially when you face an obstacle, find inner strength to try again".
>   Angela Jacobsen , OzSuperNanny & Nanny to VIP's

Take a quick check-up:
Ask yourself:
- ❓ Do you regularly show enthusiasm?
- ❓ Are you proud of your abilities?
- ❓ Do you have a happy disposition?
- ❓ Are you grateful for the positive things in your life?
- ❓ Do you know you can do it and act accordingly?
- ❓ Do you expect success?
- ❓ What is your tone of voice?
- ❓ Do you let knockbacks change your mood?
- ❓ Are you acting with desperation?
- ❓ Do you need others to pick you up often?
- ❓ Have you set goals to assist you to move forward and put you on the right path?

References:
- 📖 "Smiling Mind" app
- 📖 "Change your thinking, change your life" by Brian Tracy
- 📖 "Change your Thinking" by Sarah Edelman
- 📖 "The 7 Habits of Highly Effective People" by Stephen R. Covey
- 📖 "The Magic of Thinking Big" by David J. Schwartz
- 📖 "Six Thinking Hats" by Edward de Bono

Notes on Chapter 1

2
PRESENT YOURSELF

- "Your life only gets better when you get better". Brian Tracy
- "It doesn't matter where you are coming from. All that matters is where you are going". Brian Tracy
- "Do what you can with all you have, wherever you are". *Theodore Roosevelt*

By the end of this chapter you will have a better understanding of:
- ✓ ways to sparkle
- ✓ the value of being prepared
- ✓ how to avoid common mistakes
- ✓ how to present the best version of you

Blog:
You have approximately 7 seconds to make a good first impression in an interview.

Consequently, your personal presentation must be on point. Once this impression is made, it is very difficult to change it, so make sure you get it right!

A first impression is gained by the recruiter by engaging all of their five senses: taste, sight, touch, smell and hearing. Don't underestimate the power of all the senses working in harmony when you first meet someone.

- **Taste** (gustation)

You may think this is not relevant to an interview, but if you wear too much perfume or aftershave and then sit in a confined space in close proximity to others, it can actually be *tasted*. I have experienced this firsthand and it is not pleasant at all. When the candidate left the room on that occasion, the first thing the interviewers discussed was the discomfort of that experience and how glad they were that the candidate had left!

- **Sight** (vision)

Your appearance, presentation, hygiene, personal style, body language, posture, openness, mannerisms, demeanour, eye contact and your smile all provide visual cues to the recruiter. In just 7 seconds they have taken a mental picture that frames their opinion of you.

- **Touch** (somatosensation)

Handshakes convey a lot of information about you and getting it right can take some practice. Are they too firm, too soft, too limp, absent, sweaty, hot, cold, positioned vertically or horizontally, from above or held too long?

- **Smell** (olfaction)

Overpowering smells and odours are very distracting and should be subtle in the case of perfumes/fragrances/after shave etc. and non-existent in the case of body odours.

- **Hearing** (auditory)

The language you use in interviews must be considered. Swearing and slang should be eliminated and your tone of voice (volume, speed, pitch, mannerisms) should be moderated if possible.

So, how long should it take you to prepare to make a positive first impression?

Seven of the eight chapters in this book are dedicated to just that.

1. Motivate yourself
2. Present yourself
3. Upskill yourself
4. Amazing Application
5. Rocking Resume
6. Pre-interview
7. In Interview

It will take quite some time to work through this information and prepare yourself adequately for the task. But preparation is the key to success, so how can you place a measure on its value?

The measure of its value will be when you accept that job!

*Sometimes medical/health issues cause some of the above

conditions and cannot be eliminated/moderated. Seek help from medical or other professionals should you feel it necessary.

- **Tables of resources for Chapter 2:**

> **Table vi) Personal hygiene** is important for presenting the best version of you.
> **Table vii) Personal presentation** shows self-respect and enables you to expect it from others.

- **Tables of resources for Chapter 2:**

> **Table vi) Personal hygiene** is essential to consider when preparing for an interview. Get your body and appearance ready to convince the universe (and the employer) that you are the best candidate for the job. Put your best foot forward and respect yourself enough to present a 'sparkling' version of you. Polish your presentation overall (e.g. haircut, nails groomed) and then make a special effort just before each interview. This will keep you ready for an interview on short notice. The side benefit is you will feel better about yourself and it will show. This process does not mean you have to spend a fortune, but rather present yourself in a clean and tidy way that is suitable for the role. Below are some guidelines for making a good impression. Self-confidence will bubble up from inside.
>
> **Note: This information may seem unnecessary or obvious, however, having spent decades conducting interviews, I can assure you not everyone knows this!
>
> If you are attempting to make a good impression and eliminate anything that can distract the interviewer from concentrating on your suitability for the job, why wouldn't you do it?
>
> N.B. If any of this is not possible due to a medical condition, do the best you can to present yourself in a manner that is clean, neat and tidy. You may need to seek medical advice before making radical changes to your personal appearance.

Item	Should be:
hair	clean, trimmed, shiny, worn in a tidy style N.B. if you have dreadlocks, tie them back
mouth (teeth)	recently cleaned, polished and/or refreshed N.B. take care of your smile, it forms a big part of your first impression
eyes	recently cleaned, not bloodshot N.B. get sufficient sleep and/or use eye drops
nose	recently cleaned N.B. try to avoid excessive sniffing and have tissues on hand
ears	recently cleaned N.B. have someone check them for blackheads/whiteheads as you cannot see what others can
nails	recently cleaned, neatly manicured N.B. Trimmed, painted, nail presentation (as appropriate)
skin	recently cleaned, free of obvious blackheads/whiteheads N.B. skin conditions treated as advised by medical professionals
body piercing and tattoos	removed or covered up (as appropriate)

📄 Tables of resources for Chapter 2 continued:

Table vii) Personal presentation is essential when preparing for an interview. Just as with Personal Hygiene, put your best foot forward when it comes to your interview outfit.

What is an interview outfit?
Have one outfit that you feel really confident in. It needs to be clothing that gives you the power of knowing it looks good and feels good. Keep it freshly laundered with all pieces hanging up together, ready to go. Having the clothes ready that make you feel and look good takes away some of the stress and uncertainty of the whole process. The clothes become your official 'interview uniform', because you should *treat getting a job, as your job, until you get one.* Be mindful of not wearing the same outfit twice however, to the same organisation for subsequent interviews.

NB. If you do not have any suitable clothes/shoes/bags, op shops are a great place to start. You may also have organisations in your local area that provide clothing and accessories, for this express purpose of interviews. Referrals may be available from a "Jobactive" member.

Item	Should be:
clothes	• not too colourful • patterns that coordinate well • suitable sizes (not revealing) • in good condition (without holes or pulls) • basic and professional • appropriate for one level up from the job (e.g. labourers should not wear their work clothes) • not too dressy • clean (free of stains) • tidy and suitably presented • not smelling of smoke or body odour • suitable for the season

bags	<ul><li>not bulging with items</li><li>in good condition</li><li>looking tidy</li><li>closed or zipped up</li><li>clean (free of stains)</li></ul> N.B. have a pair of shoes, handbag, purse, wallet that coordinate with your interview outfit (described above)	
shoes	<ul><li>clean (free of stains)</li><li>in good condition</li><li>suitable for the season</li><li>suitable for your clothes</li><li>suitable sizes</li></ul>	
Perfume / aftershave/ body lotions/ hairspray etc.	applied in subtle amounts so as not to be overpowering, not too strong, remembering some people have allergies (See Pitfalls/Rejection Points above)	
make-up	<ul><li>flattering, applied subtly and not distracting</li></ul>	
reading glasses	<ul><li>clean and not in need of repairs</li><li>N.B. I have interviewed someone who had lenses so dirty they could barely see through them, and another person who had their glasses held together by Band-Aids!</li></ul>	
sunglasses	<ul><li>not to be worn during an interview</li><li>N.B. This gives the impression that there is something to hide</li></ul>	
keys	<ul><li>not in huge clumps and placed on the table or displaying inappropriate items hanging from the key rings</li></ul>	
accessories (scarves, jewellery)	<ul><li>complementing your clothes</li></ul>	

Exercise/s:

✎ Add more items to Table vi) 'Personal hygiene'.
✎ Add more items to Table vii) 'Personal presentation'.

Insider insights:
- 👍 You only have 7 seconds to make a strong first impression.
- 👍 Shoes are noticed by recruiters! If your shoes are not clean it shows your attention to detail may be lacking.
- 👍 Your car is an extension of you and may be seen by the recruiters. Clean it and tone down any outlandish components, e.g. really loud music, adornments, full of rubbish.
- 👍 If your interview is at a mealtime, you may want to eat a small snack prior to the interview to prevent your stomach from making audible noises.

Pitfalls/Rejection points:
- ✋ Overpowering odours/scents can create such a distraction that not only may the recruiters be side tracked from the selection process, but they may finish the interview quickly without properly considering the candidate. The candidate may be assumed to be a poor/uncomfortable fit into the team for the same reason.

Real life pitfall in action:
💣 *I can still smell the aftershave like it was yesterday, unrecognisable by brand but memorable none the less. When Mr Stinky entered the small, windowless interview room, there was a synchronised eye roll by all three interviewers. (Out of the candidate's vision, of course). Everyone was thinking: "Do we really have to spend half an hour locked in this perfumed prison"? Of course the unspoken answer was indeed "Yes we do". However, the interview was certainly succinct and we drew the line at any commitment beyond those 30 minutes.*

Experts in my network say:

> "The moment you walk into an interview is the moment you are judged on the job regardless of how the interview goes. Case in point ... when I attended an interview suited up, having done my research, and was faced with a panel interview of 5 civilians from different parts of the Services. I knew what they all did and answered their probing questions but it got more personal when I was able to use my experience in the Navy, my insider knowledge, as well as the research to draw on our common experiences. Informality and familiarity came over the room and we were able to share a lighthearted moment relieving the interview tension. This allowed me to relax and show the panel how much preparation I had done before the interview. I got the job".
>
>   Dave Thomas,
>   (Previously) Job Network Case
>   Manager

> "One role I went for when I didn't prepare, I got a question that I couldn't answer. I just bullsh***ed for the sake of saying something. They knew it and I didn't get the job".
>
>   Dave Thomas,
>   (Previously) Job Network Case
>   Manager

> "Create the right impression at every contact point. Your CV and Interview are important but only a part of your profile that unfolds during the recruitment and selection process. Every phone call, text, email and your social media profiles can all play an important role in your success or failure. I know of a Marketing Executive who was not offered a role because their Facebook profile was considered inappropriate for the private school they were applying to, and a discrepancy between employment dates in LinkedIn and a CV was the undoing of another candidate. Telephone manner will also be critical to some roles, while physical presentation or written communication will be more important in other positions".
>
> Peta McIver,
> Retired, taking time out to see
> Australia, previously IT Recruitment
> Consultant

Take a check-up

? Have you made the most of your 7 seconds to make a positive first impression?
? Do you have an interview outfit ready?
? Are you ready to sparkle?

References:

- What Is the Importance of Appearance on a Job Interview? By Neil Kokemuller
- Personal Appearance: Skills You Need
- "What Color is Your Parachute?" by Richard N. Bolles

Notes on Chapter 2

3
UPSKILL YOURSELF

- "You are never too old to set a new goal or dream a new dream". C. S. Lewis
- "Life isn't about finding yourself. Life is about creating yourself". George Bernard Shaw
- "Choose a job you love and you will never have to work a day in your life". Confucius

By the end of this chapter you will have a better understanding of:
- ✓ Ways to make yourself more employable
- ✓ Ideas to stay ahead and not be left behind
- ✓ What to consider when reinventing your career

Blog:
Are you prepared for change?

If there is one thing you can be sure of, it is that change is coming. In fact, the last decade has seen a more rapid rate of change than in the century preceding it. Will your chosen field still exist in the not too distant future?

Every year there are occupations that cease to exist – jobs that have been replaced by automation or that are simply no longer relevant. The flipside is that advances in technology mean new jobs and industries are constantly emerging, so much so that the jobs available in five years' time probably don't even exist yet.

With changes in:
- **Technology** (nanotechnology, robots and self-driving cars etc.)
- **The internet** (online businesses, virtual stores and remote services)
- **A desire for work-life balance** (virtual teams, an increase in part-time workers and self-employment, and socialisation of the workforce)

The job market is evolving quicker than we can keep up with it. Career paths are almost impossible to predict and we need to be more flexible, adaptable and opportunistic than ever before.

Change comes in a variety of forms and impacts all areas of our lives:

- **Political** changes in policy/funding, terrorism, contractual arrangements
- **Social** networking, media
- **Environmental** eco-friendly, climate change, global warming, responsible citizenship
- **Medical** advances and discoveries
- **Legal** loosening or tightening of restrictions
- **Economic** global interconnection, global confidence
- **Cultural** changes to adapt to internal/external forces
- **Geographical** the global community
- **Scientific** as new discoveries are made
- **Ethical** changes in acceptable/unacceptable behaviour and practices

Redundancy is increasingly commonplace as organisations struggle to adapt to change. For those employees who aren't prepared for the next step, it can have devastating consequences.

The pace of change in technology is so rapid that it is difficult to keep up. The latest electronic gadget that is supposed to make your work easier is almost outdated as soon as it is released.

Education curricula are also struggling to keep up with the rate of change. Much coursework is outdated by the time it is delivered; new rapid learning processes need to become the norm in place of traditional higher education structures.

So how do you ride the wave of change?

Discussing the automation of the workforce, a futurist recently said, "the best thing you can do as a worker is make sure you're not doing something routine and repetitive and predictable. Move into areas or things that involve working more with people or being creative".

Lifelong learning coupled with keeping your skills updated to match the shifting needs of this era, has become a necessary part of staying employable. And for business owners and leaders, the ability to predict change and stay ahead of the curve is critical. Case in point is Kodak, who discovered digital photography but remained focused on their core product – film – to the point of bankruptcy.

Change is a constant in our modern world – like it or not. To stay employable (and to stay relevant as an organisation), change needs to be embraced whilst continuously expanding knowledge and skillsets. The expression, "You don't know what you don't know" may never have been as relevant as it is now!

Tables of resources for Chapter 3:

> **Table viii) Choose a career** taking into account, interests, talents, skills etc.
> **Table ix) Employability skills** are valuable skills that appear in training packages.
> **Table x) Personal attributes** gives you a point of difference to other candidates.
> **Table xi) Upskill yourself** to be well equipped and ready.
> **Table xii) Transferrable skills** are life skills obtained anytime and anywhere.

SECTION 3. The Chapters

Tables of resources for Chapter 3:

Table viii) Choose a career list your interests, experience and ambition. By identifying these things you can become clearer on how they may impact your career choices. Use this information in conjunction with "The Job Guide" to determine and research your career options.

Dreaming big is an important part of career planning – we *should* reach for the stars. As children we are told that we can be anything we want to be, and it is true – as long as you put in the required work, remain persistent and never give up. Things to consider:
- Set yourself realistic aspirations (some industries may only employ a very small number of people e.g. foreign correspondents. Others may only be available in certain parts of the world, e.g. becoming an astronaut.)
- What are the emerging fields/industries?
- What fields of work are dying out?
- What are your true strengths and are there skills that naturally align?

There are many stories of people who have reached their career goal despite barriers to success, so don't be deterred. Use these as inspiration to reach your own goals.

Interests
What are your hobbies?
What do you spend your spare money on?
What gifts do you buy for yourself?
What subjects did you study at school?

Experience
What hobbies/community work have you done that you enjoyed?
What previous jobs have you had where you felt fulfilled?
When were you feeling good about your work?
When did you receive accolades, bonuses, recognition at work?

Ambition What new areas are you interested in? What promotions are you seeking? What alternate fields interest you? Understand your level of ambition? What drives you? (Money, power, stability, security, knowing your place, using initiative etc.)	
Ideas to explore	

Tables of resources for Chapter 3 continued:

Table ix) Employability skills is a list of items that are recognised as skills that will assist you into employment. These skills are used extensively throughout both education and training, and are qualities and abilities rather than direct employment-based skills.

Skill	Element
Communication: … that contributes to productive and harmonious relations between both employees and customers	• Listening and understanding • Speaking clearly and directly
Teamwork: … that contributes to productive working relationships and outcomes	• Working as an individual and as a member of a team • Identifying the strengths of other team members
Problem solving: … that contributes to productive outcomes	• Developing creative, innovative solutions • Applying a range of strategies to problem solving
Initiative and enterprise: … that contributes to innovative outcomes	• Adapting to new situations • Being a creative thinker

SECTION 3. The Chapters

Planning and organising: ... that contributes to long and short-term strategic planning	• Being resourceful • Taking initiative and making decisions
Self-management: ... that contributes to employee satisfaction and growth	• Having a personal vision and goal • Taking responsibility
Learning ability: ... that contributes to ongoing improvement and expansion in employee and company operations and outcomes	• Managing own learning • Contributes to the learning community in the workplace
Technology: ... that contributes to effective execution of tasks	• Having a range of basic IT skills • Using IT to organise data and communicate

▤ Tables of resources for Chapter 3 continued:

Table x) Personal attributes is a list of adjectives that you can link to examples taken from your work history and experiences for use in interview.

Personal attributes	Demonstration of these attributes in a previous job
Loyalty	
Honesty & integrity	
Commitment	
Enthusiasm	
Reliability	

Personal presentation	
Common sense	
Positive self-esteem	
Sense of humour	
Attitude to work/life balance	
Ability to deal with pressure	
Motivation	
Adaptability	

▤ **Tables of resources for Chapter 3 continued:**

> **Table xi) Upskill yourself** is a list of the hierarchy of education through Secondary Education into Tertiary Education. You can use this list to identify how to upskill yourself via increasing your education level. (Note the differences between states).

SECTION 3. The Chapters

Year 10	State	Abbreviation
Senior Secondary school: VCE	VIC	• Victorian Certificate of Education
VCAL	VIC	• Victorian Certificate of Advanced Learning
HSC	NSW	• Higher School Certificate
QCE	QLD	• Queensland Certificate of Education
SACE	SA	• South Australian Certificate of Education
WACE	WA	• West Australian Certificate of Education
TCE	TAS	• Tasmanian Certificate of Education
ACTCE	ACT	• Year 12 Certificate
NTCET	NT	• Northern Territory Certificate of Education & Training
Academic Qualifications		
Certificate I		
Certificate II		
Certificate III		
Certificate IV		
Diploma		
Associate Degree & Advanced Diploma		
Bachelor Degree		
Graduate Diploma, Graduate Certificate & Bachelor Honours Degree		
Master's Degree		
Doctoral Degree		

📄 Tables of resources for Chapter 3 continued:

Table xii) Transferrable skills is a list of skills that can be obtained from life experience and not necessarily from work history. These skills are just as valid in contributing positively towards a work environment as direct experience in a similar role can be. Using transferrable skills adds weight to your application in the situation where your work experience is minimal or you've been absent from the workforce for extended periods of time. It recognises that we gather many skills from life outside of work that can be "transferred" into the workplace.

We all possess these portable skills so it's important to identify them. For example, it can be highly relevant that you have been president of a school council if you are applying for a leadership role.

Do not underestimate the value of transferrable skills. We all use them every day to undertake tasks and duties. If you have been out of the workforce for some time, it is especially important to draw on these skills and recognise they form part of the package you bring to a new employer.

Skills	**Ways to include them on your resume:**
interpersonal	• team player
organisation	• meeting deadlines
leadership	• supervising staff • delegation
communication	• training • preparing publications
motivation	• works well independently
prioritisation	• time management
listening	• counselling
analytics	• writing technical reports
research	• gathering data for a project

Exercise:
- 🖉 Add your ideas to Table viii) 'Choose a career' to start exploring career options.
- 🖉 Add examples to Table x) 'Personal attributes'.
- 🖉 Add more Elements to Table xi) 'Upskill yourself' – Ref: www.education.vic.gov.au
- 🖉 Add examples of transferrable skills and ways to include them on your resume to Table xii) 'Transferrable Skills'.

Insider insights:
- 👍 Do some further reading on relevant subjects.
- 👍 Use *The Job Guide* as it has highly valuable information.
- 👍 Online career guidance programs can be very useful.
- 👍 Do regular stock takes of your skills and experience. Look for gaps.

Pitfalls /Rejection Points:
- ✋ Being an eternal student with sketchy work history can raise red flags for your ability to commit to any one thing.
- ✋ Having lots of unfinished learning opportunities (courses, degrees etc.) may suggest you give up easily.
- ✋ By applying for jobs that clearly state compulsory pre-requisites that you do not possess.

Real life pitfall in action:
- 💥 *Why the unsuccessful candidate (let's call her 'Deluded') applied for the role of Management Accountant, despite her not having the required degree that was stipulated in the advertisement, was unfathomable. Her previous experience was a solid history of unskilled factory work. Although her aspirations were admirable, the four years it would have taken her to qualify for this role were outside our hiring timeline!*

Experts in my network say:

> "Lifelong learning is what we all do now to ensure we keep up to date with current trends and information. Sometimes the word learning can make people's eyes glaze over, so it's best to think about it as simply keeping up to date with new information, new technology, new systems, new styles of working, etc. Other ways of upskilling yourself may involve formal training, learning or education which means enrolling, paying fees and attending (online, face-to-face, off campus, etc.) completing the required work and receiving a certificate or qualification. Using what you have learnt is the key. When you have proactively upskilled yourself then you implement the new skills, it becomes very obvious to others; they see you using new skills, language, or behaviours. Upskilling is really just keeping yourself fresh and relevant in your workplace or industry".
>
> Mary Tresize-Brown, Development Officer – Schools & Community SE LLEN

> "You are never too old to change career path"
>
> Angela Jacobsen, OzSuperNanny & Nanny to VIP's

Take a quick check-up:
- **?** It is time to assess what interests, skills, attributes and experience you currently have.
- **?** What could make you more employable and put you on the right path?
- **?** Is there anything you can finish that you have already begun?
- **?** Are there any relevant short courses that you can do?
- **?** Is there anything that would complement a skill you already have?
- **?** Are you connected to suitable networks/social media?
- **?** Have you proactively grown your networks to connect you further?
- **?** Do you need to find a new direction?

References:
- 💻 Career voyage and other similar surveys can help you identify occupations
- 💻 The Job Guide: a resource provided by the Federal Government
- 💻 Transferrable skills
- 💻 Career Counsellors to help you explore areas of interest
- 📖 "Who Moved My Cheese?" by Spencer Johnson
- 📖 "What Color is Your Parachute?" by Richard N. Bolles

Notes on Chapter 3

4
AMAZING APPLICATION

- "I like good strong words that mean something ... " Louisa May Alcott
- "The ability to simplify means to eliminate the unnecessary so the necessary may speak". Hans Hofmann
- "Don't repeat yourself. It's not only repetitive, it's redundant and people have heard it before". Lemony Snicket

By the end of this chapter you will have a better understanding of:
- ✓ how to gain the attention of the reader
- ✓ ways to make your Application/Cover Letter sing
- ✓ why omissions are as important as inclusions
- ✓ when to submit a 'Selection Criteria'

💻 Blog:

The purpose of the Application Letter is to peak the employer's interest enough to make them want to meet you and learn more. If you want your resume to be read, then start by making it stand out from the rest, pointing to the things that make you suitable for the job.

Start by clearly setting the intention.

If the recruiter is bored, or can't immediately see a reason to read further, they will give up on your application before it's really even started. You then exit the process and get a rejection letter.

I know this happens – because I have done it myself many times.

You need help with your Application letter if you:

- Simply repeat information from your resume
- Can't contain the information to one page
- Just don't know where to begin

The structure should be obvious: it needs to have a beginning, middle and end.

The *beginning* is brief and factual, detailing what you are applying for by clearly restating the correct title (including reference numbers if they are in the advertisement).

The *middle* is the guts of your application and should highlight relevant aspects of your experience that relate directly to the role. This is where most people go wrong. This section should be no longer than three or four short paragraphs.

The *end* is a brief upbeat and confident conclusion to the letter anticipating a positive response.

▤ **Tables of resources for Chapter 4:**

> **Table xiii) Where to find jobs** helps you to look in the right places.
> **Table xiv) Amazing Application inclusions** shows you it is equally important to omit things.
> **Table xv) Structure of Amazing Application** gives you the wow factor.
> **Table xvi) Ways to stand out** (self-explanatory).
> **Table xvii) Selection Criteria should be**: a list of inclusions.

Tables of resources for Chapter 4:

Table xiii) Where to find jobs is a list of places to look for jobs specifically identifying the difference between "Advertised Jobs" and jobs in "The Hidden Job Market". Approximately 80% of jobs are in the hidden job market! You will have much better odds of success if you tap into this part of the market and not just focus on the advertised positions.

Jobactive	available to unemployment benefit recipients at certain stages, who are connected to a "Jobactive Provider" (refer to your designated Consultant) jobsearch.gov.au
Advertised jobs:	
online	job search sites: use classified careers sites such as SEEK or CareerOne as they are a good place to see multiple jobs available in a particular field
websites	Most organisations advertise vacancies on their own website. Make a list of those you would like to work for and keep checking in to see what jobs they have available
newspapers	National, state and local papers are still a good place to find jobs. Learn which days specialise in your industry and also when there are seasonal high recruitment periods
agencies	Let someone else "do the walking" for you. Register with agencies that specialise in your industry and make the most of their contacts and repeat clients
Hidden Job Market:	
social media	Join local/industry job search groups, use LinkedIn to connect with employees of organisations you are interested in, join the conversations about industry issues in online forums.

networking	expand your networks to include professional contacts: make it known you are seeking work and the specific type talk to people in the networks that you want to work in become known in the arena you seek to work in
networks	We all have many networks – work them! Sports groups, church groups, parents of your children's friends, family friends, associations you belong to etc.
in person	making a memorable first impression – 'on the spot' advantage
by phone	making a memorable first impression, dependant on size of business/company/ organisation: use your mobile contacts
cold calling	in person or by phone as is appropriate for your industry: previous employers, new businesses, all major employers in your area, all employers in chosen industry in your target area
professional associations	online and publications: know where to find advertisements
expos	know the annual calendar for expos in your local and capital city
open days	know when these occur for any businesses/ companies/organisations you are interested in and attend
grants in your area	know who has received a grant to manage a project that may interest you
advertisers	who is advertising their business/company/ organisation in your area that may need new staff and contact as appropriate
email	email your list of contacts to let them know you're available.

Tables of resources for Chapter 4 continued:

Table xiv) Amazing Application inclusions: is a list of the essential elements of an application and how to make it effective.	
concise	• every word that is used is necessary to convey the required meaning • no repetition of the same words
professional	• take language cues from the advertisement and position description • choose words that are used in the business/company/organisation that you are applying for
appropriate	• complementary to your resume • not too long and not too short (follow the formula outlined in this chapter)
interesting	• provide a glimpse into your personality • avoid starting every sentence with "I" • don't repeat the same information • use cadence that allows for flow
leading tone	• elude to what's to come (in the resume) without giving it all away (hook the reader in to want to meet you) • elude to your successful progression to the next step without being over confident
accurate	• data • spelling • proofread several times • proofread by someone else • details of recruiter/organisation
summarising	• a flash report of your key experiences and relevant skills
mirroring	• use keywords from the advertisement and/or position description • be aware of the language used in the advertisement
grammatical	• pertain to syntax i.e. structure • accurate spelling • use words in the correct tense • correct context
individual	• ensure you stand out from other candidates

▤ Tables of resources for Chapter 4 continued:

Table xv) Structure of Amazing Application. Your application must include certain items that are detailed in a considered manner, with examples.

Remember you are being judged on your *attention to detail* in every aspect of the application and none more so than in the application, as it is the first impression that you make on the recruiter.

To help improve your chances of making it to the next stage in the recruitment process take care with the small things, because they make a big difference. This is especially important when the job has *attention to detail* listed as a 'required skill'!

▤ Tables of resources for Chapter 4 continued:

Table xvi) Ways to stand out details some specific ways to make the most of your opportunity to impress when preparing an application for employment.

When you have a lot of competition and want your application to work hard for you, there are creative ways to prepare your application. The choices you make should be appropriate and match the job/industry. You may feel some of these are risky but sometimes acting outside the box is the thing that gets you invited to interview.

paper	• watermarks on the paper can be effective e.g. waves for a shipping line • traditional paper for e.g. funeral industry • logos of the organisation you are applying to • coloured e.g. matching a logo of the organisation

inclusions	• Some strategies I have seen that have been effective: • staple item to application e.g. confectionary for marketing/advertising • staple item to application e.g. tea bag, cuppa soup asking Recruiter to take a break while reading your application • include a photo e.g. modelling, acting
style	• have clean lines that make it easy to read • use white space for emphasis • match the style of the industry e.g. very formal for accounting • vary the opening of the letter from the standard format e.g. industries recruiting young people with initiative and big ideas don't necessarily want to see 'Dear Sir'
format	• Make a score card of the requirements/your matches so it's easy to see at a glance how suitable you are
text	• emphasise keywords or phrases, mirroring the original advertisement or position description • use keywords from the Mission Statement of the business/company/organisation
tone	• when the ad asks for a good sense of humour, they have thrown out the gauntlet so go for it • when the ad is dry and very professional then that is your queue to reply in the same tone/flavour/manner
delivery	• Email (usual manner) • By the post (takes longer but if you know the closing date and you can meet the deadline and you want to use one of the strategies listed above it may be the most effective. Send an email version too for ease of sharing by the recruiter, and note you have done this.) • Hand delivered (allows for making an impression and checking out the venue. Send an email version too for ease of sharing by the recruiter, and note you have done this.)

▤ **Tables of resources for Chapter 4 continued:**

Table xvii) Selection Criteria should be: a list of the methods of how to prepare an effective application when Selection Criteria is required.
This should be prepared *only* when expressly asked for in the advertisement. Source the specific criterion to be addressed from the advertisement or more often, the Position Description (N.B. be aware of specific use for difference industries e.g. The Public Service, Education etc.)

Method:	
reproduce the exact Selection Criteria	• copy and paste from the original document (to avoid errors) • repeat the question to make it clearer for the reader
plan it	• bullet point the content you wish to include with examples of your work history that are relevant to each point • clear, easy to read, use italics and bolding for emphasis
identify	• examples (or several examples) for each criteria • provide a range of multiple examples from different jobs, this shows a depth of experience
set out items spread over one or two pages	• make good use of white spaces for emphasis
write it	• don't rush it, know the closing date and plan out the time accordingly
sleep on it/revisit/improve it	• it is amazing how different examples or descriptions come to you on a new day
proofread	• this is your last chance to get it right

use a second pair of eyes to proofread it	• maybe ask one of your referees (if appropriate), this has the double benefit of making them more familiar with the role you have applied for and will prepare them for the job of providing a reference for you

Exercise/s:

🖋 Add your ideas to Table xvi) 'Ways to stand out' for the industry you want to work in

Insider insights:

- 👍 AIDA Model: Gain the reader's **attention**, stimulate their **interest,** awaken their **desire** and spur them into **action.**
- 👍 Use white space thoughtfully to make the body of the letter have more impact.
- 👍 Every word needs to work as part of the letter, if it is redundant, leave it out.
- 👍 Limit the letter to one page for maximum impact.

Pitfalls/Rejection points:

- 👋 When the letter is so long that the reader has lost their desire to learn any more about you and certainly isn't wanting to meet you.
- 👋 When grammar, spelling, format are so distracting the reader cannot find a reason to continue.
- 👋 Poor attention to detail says you care little about what you're doing (it is assumed this will be how you perform your job too).
- 👋 N.B. Some Recruiters screen applications electronically, this means if you don't mention the keywords then you are screened out automatically.
- 👋 When the letter is simply a rehash of information already on the resume.

Real life pitfall in action:

💣 *There was definitely skill in 'cutting and pasting' but that was about it! The content in the Application Letter was exactly the same as that in the resume. It wasn't impressive and certainly wasn't going to secure Ms 'Snip and Glue' a place on the shortlist.*

Experts in my network say:

> ➤ "The 30 second and 60 second commercial are very popular tools. Have you ever been asked "What do you do for a living?", or "So, tell me a little about yourself". The answer to those questions is your 30 second and 60 second commercial, or your 'elevator pitch'. You should be prepared and practice these regularly. Now, you find yourself in an elevator on your way to your interview when the CEO for that company gets in the elevator. There are a few floors remaining before you get off. The CEO asks if you are a candidate for the position that they have been advertising. You respond with a confident "Yes". The CEO asks you why they should hire you. You respond with your tailored 30 second commercial and whatever you tell the CEO is what you should write down and use to form the foundation of your application letter".
>   Rodney Malloy,
>   Small business owner, IT Consulting Services

> ➤ "Ensure that the application letter is about you being able to perform in the job, it is not about you personally. The reader does not need to know about your friends and family and why you enjoy taking long walks on the beach".
>   Rodney Malloy
>   Small business owner, IT Consulting Services

> "A good portion of your time should be spent dedicated to the hidden job market, through networking, direct marketing, letters to organisations and cold calling".
>
> Gaye Kidder, Managing Director, LEC Recruitment

> "Read your application AT LEAST ONCE before submitting! It may be a good idea to get someone else to review it too – a fresh pair of eyes, who may pick up something you've missed. If possible, send your application a day after you've written it ... this should remove any emotion you had when you first wrote it and you may find you need to alter it slightly as a result.
>
> Be polite, professional and use correct etiquette ... or mirror the language used in the advertisement (e.g. some quirky marketing or designer companies are less formal and take a different and less 'dull' approach).
>
> For goodness sake, spell correctly!
>
> Make sure you really want the job ... please don't just apply because you need any job. This wastes everyone's time, including yours!"
>
> Linda Perrins,
> Previously Correspondence Clerk/
> Customer Complaints Officer

Take a quick check-up:
- **?** Do you know when you have written enough in your Application/Cover Letter?
- **?** What can you include/attach something to your application to make it catchy and clever without it being lame?
- **?** Have you done enough research about the business/company/organisation you are applying to that allows you to talk their language?

References:
- jobsearch.gov.au
- Application/Cover Letter Templates

N.B. Everybody has different advice for how to prepare an Application Letter! The preceding chapter details the formula that I have found to work for me both as a recruiter, hiring manager and applicant. There is no shortage of other material available online and you should undertake further reading if you want to, just be forewarned that it may confuse instead of clarifying. I firmly believe in my "Eight Essential Elements to Employment" so consequently, have not provided any further references on the subject.

Notes on Chapter 4

5
ROCKING RESUME

- "I believe more in the scissors than I do in the pencil". Truman Capote
- "The whole is greater than the sum of its parts". Aristotle
- "Simplicity is the ultimate sophistication". Leonardo De Vinci

By the end of this chapter you will have a better understanding of:
- ✓ How to join the market
- ✓ How to choose the role
- ✓ What structure and format to use in your resume

Blog:
What is the purpose of a resume?

Building a resume is a lot like building a house. You need a purposeful design (format), suitable materials (font) and the right species of wood (words) to make a sturdy structure. It is just as important to know what to leave out, as it is to know what to include.

Your resume is *not* a story, it is a summary of your details, skills and experience that is relevant to a particular job. Don't start right at the beginning and tell the reader everything you've ever done. You do, however, need to let your personality shine through the words on the page.

Recently when preparing a resume for a client, I realised that *letting go* of very old work history can be a painful experience. To hold onto redundant job history and lengthy descriptions of meaningless responsibilities is to live in a beautiful new house filled with clutter. Free yourself to accept a new future by letting go of the irrelevant past.

So what is the purpose of a resume, I hear you ask? The sole purpose is <u>to get you an interview!</u>

Does your resume need to sing a new song? Contact me to discuss your specific requirements.

SECTION 3. The Chapters

▤ **Tables of resources for Chapter 5:**

Table xviii) Format of a Rocking Resume make the format clean, professional and consistent.
Table ixx) Structure of a Rocking Resume should complement the application and not be a further distraction.

▤ **Tables of resources for Chapter 5 continued:**

Table xviii) Format of a Rocking Resume outlines all aspects to be considered when compiling a resume. This is specifically the way to format the document rather than the content within it.

Format	Should:
General	<ul><li>List duties in correct order, main ones first</li><li>list education and employment in chronological order</li><li>-education: begin with oldest and finish with the most recent</li><li>-employment history: begin with the most current position and work backwards (unless your experience is more extensive than 10 years and you want to emphasise specific work history)</li><li>not too long or too short (eliminate unnecessary words)</li><li>approximately 3 pages is a good guide</li><li>only include *all* of your work history if you are young with little experience</li><li>only include the last ten years' experience. If you want to juggle the order of work history slightly to emphasise relevant experience, remove the dates</li><li>don't include dates of employment if you have big gaps and you don't want to explain them (not much experience and no dates screams unemployment or incarceration)</li><li>don't include a reason for leaving each job</li><li>use consistent formatting e.g. font, spacing, bold or italicised</li></ul>

Layout	• Ensure all content is either left aligned or fully justified. Whatever you decide, ensure it is consistent throughout (left hand justification is standard)
Font/size	• Use modern fonts (especially if you are older and don't want it to be obvious). Typically a sans serif font such as Arial or Calibri. • Choose a font that is appropriate to the role and organisation. Use a font size that is standard i.e. 11 or 12 • Consider a larger font for your name as a heading • e.g. Confidential resume of Jane Doe
Underscore	• Don't use underlining for emphasis as it suggests a link to more information, particularly when being read on screen
Capitalisation	• Capitals can be used for emphasis but be consistent through the document and ensure it can't be perceived as 'shouting' at the reader
Page numbers	• Page numbers help for reference if there are multiple interviewers and also add to the professionalism of your document
Footer	• Bottom left 'Confidential Resume of Jane Doe' in small font and italics adds a professional touch and can be a useful reference
Italics	• Use for emphasis or to show contrast
Bold	• Use for emphasis
Heading Style	• Various styles can work equally well. Decide on a consistent way to emphasise the important items, such as sections or headings, and follow it though the entire document

SECTION 3. The Chapters

▤ **Tables of resources for Chapter 5 continued:**

Table ixx) Structure of a Rocking Resume is a listing of each heading you can use in your resume, the information contained under that heading and what to include in that section. It also gives you a classic order to record the information. This order can be altered depending on emphasis required for the specific application.

Heading	Descriptor	Information	Instructions
Personal	Data Information Details Summary	Name DOB Address Email Mobile & Landline	• Use full name • No date of birth (unless it is a positive) • Correct format street address • Email account with appropriate name (if not set up a new one) • Inward phone calls: • check recorded message is suitable; always answer appropriately; prepare others in the house for incoming calls

Education	History Details Background Qualifications and Training Credentials Summary Certifications	Academic Secondary & Tertiary Qualifications Courses Certificates Licences	• Include courses, even if not completed, where relevant. (You have still acquired some of the learning) • Include subjects: • highlighting any with exceptional results, awards etc. (especially if there is not much work history) • Include grades, particularly if they're great! • Use correct name • Include level and correct title
Extra-curricular	Experience Affiliations Associations Memberships Involvements Activities Summary	Professional Community Volunteer Personal Interests Political	• Use as a heading when there are a lot of things you participated in as part of your education • Unpaid work is as important as paid work, particularly if you can demonstrate a certain skillset that is relevant

SECTION 3. The Chapters

Career	Goals Objectives Summary Experience Background Skills Aspirations Profile	A summary of your career with particular emphasis on its relevance to the job you are applying for	• Use this for a professional job with opportunities for advancement to show: 1. you have considered it 2. you know what you want 3. your goals are consistent with the employer • Use to stand out from other applicants • Use this to interest your reader • (Don't use standard "Job Agency terminology" or you will look too similar to that of others, so, if you use a resume template be mindful of altering it to highlight your individuality)

Employment / Work	Goals Objectives History Summary Experience Background Skills Aspirations Profile	Professional Freelance Technical Career Executive Voluntary: Aid work/ Humanitarian work/ Community work	• Use consistent descriptions across all jobs, but don't repeat yourself • Use politically correct terminology (especially job titles) • Use the best description of your job title even if your employer called it something else (this may make it sound more modern or more in keeping with the current job market and the role you are applying for) • Put jobs in historical order starting with the most recent and work backwards • Change the order of jobs without dates if the last job you had is not the most relevant and/or was a while ago

SECTION 3. The Chapters

- If you completely switch the order around to show the most relevant experience first you can also include a summary of experience before the employment history. Ensure it is not confusing (use your second pair of eyes to check)

- Use the correct name of your previous employers

- Bold the thing you want the recruiter to notice first, i.e. the title or the company, then do it consistently across all jobs

- Use quotes in the resume especially if light on experience (these may be from a written reference, a performance review, a farewell card, etc.)

				• Include unpaid work, it is still work and it adds to your skills base
				• Include Work for the Dole
				• Include work done overseas
				• When including this type of work be sensitive to the cause you worked for and the goals of the organisation you are applying to
				• If you have minimal work history, include school activities like working in canteen, babysitting, selling tickets for sporting clubs, etc.

SECTION 3. The Chapters

Skills Key Competencies/ Core Competencies	Summary Information Details Profile	Team work Mediation Negotiation Running meetings It is better to list the things that are not included in the responsibilities under work history	• Skills should only be included if they really add weight to the experience you're discussing. • Agencies often use skills as fillers and therefore they are often standardised and not very accurate • Are the skills you are including relevant to the position you are applying for?
Computer	Knowledge Background Skills Packages Languages Proficiencies Experience Summary	Programming Technical Packages Languages Platforms	• Highlight the computer language if it is the same as the advertisement to mirror the employer's expectations
Publications	Summary Profile History	Thesis Publications: Research Papers Books Journal articles Short stories Technical manual Newspaper columns Online Blogs Websites etc.	• include opening sentences to major pieces of work as appropriate to the job you are applying for (this will grab the attention of the recruiter) • include web addresses to point to your work • include hyperlinks as appropriate

103

Accomplishments		Career milestones Awards Prizes Sporting/ Literary/ Science, etc.	• Use this section to highlight anything you have achieved that is noteworthy
Hobbies	Hobbies & Interests		• Don't put too many (unless it is relevant to job, as it looks like you are more interested in your time off than work) • List them in order of interest and/or time spent doing them • Don't put all pastimes that are solo (not good for team jobs) • Show at least one activity that is a team pursuit (if you can) • Put things that are true or you are actually interested in (beware the chatty interviewer who shares a hobby or uses it as an icebreaker) • If asked, show passion about a hobby

SECTION 3. The Chapters

			• Inexperienced interviewers will see similarities in you via hobbies and may favour you for the job e.g. you follow the same Football Team • This can provide a glimpse into your personality
Referee/s	Summary Details	Testimonials References Referees	• If they are requested definitely put them • Consider putting "referees available on request" (gives you more control) • Prepare the referees with as much info as appropriate • Provide referees with a Position Description, info about business/ company/ organisation • Discuss your level of interest in the job with passion • Keep referee details accurate and up to date • List referees in the appropriate order (most suitable first or who you want contacted)

105

- If you have referees that know the interviewer or have a relationship with the business/ company/ organisation, put them first
- Include no more than three
- Usually the first two are contacted and the third is an emergency
- Include quotes from written or verbal references after the contact details to highlight areas that would be valued by an Employer
- Include referee's:
  · Name
  · Business Name
  · Correct title (or their title when they supervised you)
  · Mobile number
- Don't wear out your referees
- Use different referees for different roles, choosing the most suitable

					<ul><li>Tell your referee the important aspects of the job and how interested you are in it, so they can accurately talk about your experience (this is to your advantage)</li><li>Ask your referees to advise you if they are called, as an offer may be imminent</li><li>Ask your referee to engage the interviewer and see what they can learn about how many candidates are being checked or any other relevant information that helps update you on the status of the recruitment process.</li></ul>

Exercise/s:
- Add information to the General section of Table xviii) 'Format of a Rocking Resume' that you feel is relevant or key points you wish to use.
- Underline specific points you wish to use in Table ixx) 'Structure of a Rocking Resume.'

Insider insights:
- Proofread.
- Provide no reason to be screened out.
- Make good use of every word.
- Only use a photo on the resume if it is relevant to the job you're applying for. For example modelling or acting.

- 👍 Put the anticipated contact into you mobile for phone calls that may catch you unawares so you can react appropriately.
- 👍 Read your current document and see how much it tells you about, your age, your lack of experience, depth of experience, ability to stay in a job, what is important to you i.e. hobbies, how much time and care you took preparing the document, how much you want a job, how professional you are, attention to detail, how verbose you are, how tidy it is, how easy to read it is, how long or short it is. And finally, is it the best reflection of you as a person and potential employee. This is the objective way it will be screened by the Recruiter.
- 👍 Use appropriate names for saving a document if you are sending it electronically.
- 👍 Are you prepared for the social media 'check-up' that will inevitably take place prior to interview?

Pitfalls/Rejection points:
- ✋ Leaving off important information.
- ✋ Including too much information.
- ✋ Poor attention to detail.
- ✋ Choosing a job/ industry/field /opportunity that is wrong for you.
- ✋ Sending the information in a format or size that doesn't match the request.
- ✋ Not applying online when requested to do so.
- ✋ Incorrectly addressed.

Real life pitfall in action:
💣 *It appeared like any other application, until I opened it and saw it. It was addressed to Mrs Pauline Visser, but then the letter began: Dear Sir… Let's call this applicant 'Whoops-a-Daisy!*

Experts in my network say:

> "Reading a resume should not be like reading a memoir. It must however, still be a darn good read. It needs to accurately represent what you've done, and be an account of what you're good at, BUT it also needs to hold the reader's interest and pique their curiosity. Give your potential employer a reason to pick up the phone and invite you in for interview. Don't be same-same. Your resume is the entrée – if it isn't great you won't get a chance to share the main meal"
>
> Jo Johnson
> The Content Coach

Take a quick check-up:
- **?** Do you start lots of sentences with "I"?
- **?** Does every job repeat the same responsibilities?
- **?** Do you put 'reason for leaving' on some jobs and not others?
- **?** Is your email address suitable for this purpose?
- **?** Does your resume contradict information on social media?

References:
- jobsearch.gov.au
- resume templates
- CareerOne

Notes on Chapter 5

6
PRE INTERVIEW

- "Knowledge is a powerful weapon, arm yourself well with it before going to do battle". George R. R. Martin
- "By failing to prepare you are preparing to fail". Benjamin Franklin
- "Research is creating new knowledge". Neil Armstrong

By the end of this chapter you will have a better understanding of:
- ✓ How to turn weaknesses into strengths
- ✓ Why you should record your applications
- ✓ Ways to prepare for an interview that will build your confidence

Blog:
Ready, set, go! When does the interview actually begin?

The answer to that question is not as straight forward as you may think. My advice is that you should act in a manner that would be appropriate for the interview from the moment you leave home.

Why?

Once upon a time on a dreary winter's morning in Melbourne, I left Flinders Street Station and made my way to the address of my interview. I had arrived early and after much anticipation and significant preparation, coffee was what I needed. There was a welcoming looking café right opposite, enticing me in out of the cold wind. A chance to give me time to gather my thoughts and breathe. It was during the quiet moments when I was mentally preparing myself, thinking through the research I had done and referring to my notes (detailing the Mission Statement of the Organisation), that it happened.

Three customers arrived at the table next to me, bustling in from the cold and settling with their morning 'pick me up 'coffee, chatting about their busy day ahead. Their mundane conversation was insignificant to me as I continued to prepare for my big moment. My thoughts went to being conscious of my breathing and trying to slow it down so as to appear calm and collected – neither of which was what I was actually feeling. I visualised answering questions confidently that were met with pleasing reactions from my interviewers.

Then somebody blew in from the windy street and asked to join me at my table. As there was space and I sat their alone, I nodded with approval. We were two strangers together in the midst of the morning coffee desperation of the busy Melbourne working scene. My new friend was enquiring of my reason to be where I was so I said I was attending an interview. "Likewise", I was told, and instantly our common experience bonded us. After some general banter about what was before us, we braved the cold and moved together onto the elevator and into our (group) interview room.

After a very short time, and to our amazement, the three café patrons who sat at the next table, who no doubt heard our conversation clearly, introduced themselves to the room as the interviewers. After a moment of trepidation trying to recall exactly what I had said in that busy café within their earshot, I felt pleased I had stuck to my well-honed practice of expecting anything and behaving in a manner that befits an interviewee from the moment of leaving my home. Phew!

Table of resources for Chapter 6:

> **Table xx) Turn weaknesses into** strengths and never fear these questions again!
> **Table xxi) Record of applications** is often overlooked but is a valuable step.

🗏 Table of resources for Chapter 6 continued:

Table xx) Turn weaknesses into strengths is a list of some typical 'weaknesses' that can be turned around and made into strengths. The question, "What are your weaknesses"? is a common one in interviews and there are good and bad ways to answer it. This 'turnaround' strategy can be used effectively when you know how.

Before the interview, identify several 'weaknesses' that relate directly to the candidate requirements from the Position Description of the position you are being interviewed for. (Trying to identify suitable weaknesses on the spot is fraught with danger.) Then with the right mindset, you can learn to view each of the weaknesses as simply the opposite side of the same coin.

When applying for a job you can imagine what qualities the employer would be looking for in their employee and use those qualities to prepare your list of strengths and weaknesses.

Never discuss your weaknesses without having first worked out how you could turn them into positive attributes. Here are some examples of how to make all of your qualities work for you, even your weaknesses.

Weakness	Strength
Slow to make decisions	This becomes a strength when you explain how taking your time to weigh up all of the facts makes for a more considered decision. Consequently, there is no need for damage control, because the decision wasn't made in isolation (or in haste) but instead was made with the understanding of the ripple effect across other teams/areas of the business.

Not good with numbers	Always using a calculator and double-checking when working with numbers means less errors. This also means that words are more of a strength and that can be more important when working in a team.
Not a people person	Having friends and socialising outside of work is one thing but being too chatty on the job can be counterproductive. Many roles are well suited to people who prefer to work alone such as those requiring deep concentration, working with computers, research etc. (Take care with this one if you are applying to be part of a team or in a customer-facing role).
Get bored with routine tasks	This may be a sign that you are capable of much more than the job you are doing and can be utilised to the advantage of your employer. You may still be able to perform the role you are in whilst taking on more challenging tasks, which benefits both parties. Increased job satisfaction means more productivity. You are eager to learn new things and to be stretched beyond your existing tasks.
Becomes unmotivated without feedback	This is gold to your new employer. You are telling them what motivates you, which saves them the time to discover this therefore they'll get the best out of you from day one. You are being proactive by seeking feedback, which informs your progress in the role. This will allow you to adjust your performance and make improvements where necessary.

Table of resources for Chapter 6 continued:

Table xxi) Record of applications is a record of the applications you have made.

This is a useful process to undertake for all job seekers, not just those who are required to do so for Centrelink purposes. By keeping a reference list of the jobs you've applied for, it reduces your chance of forgetting the important details of each and therefore possibly making a mistake. Each employer should feel like theirs is the only job you have applied for and that you are really interested in it – even if you have applied for many others. No potential employer wants to know that you can't immediately recall the details of their job if called for interview.

A record of applications is also a good way to look back on how many jobs you are applying for without success, allowing you to identify potential impediments or patterns in getting to the next step. If you are applying for lots of jobs and never being called to attend an interview, for example, the problem is in the application.

Date	Job title	Employer	Contact person	Contact details	$	Rating
1/7/16	Accounts clerk	ABC Finance	Joe Bloggs	jbloggs@abc.com 1300 1122	45k	4/5

Exercise/s:

- Add more examples to Table xx) 'Turn weaknesses into strengths'.
- Add 5 jobs you have recently applied to Table xxi) 'Record of applications'.

Insider insights:
- Become known before the interview (in a positive light).
- Know what motivates you.
- Research buzzwords for the industry so you can 'talk the talk'.
- Practice deep breathing prior to the interview to gain clarity, reduce confusion and anxiety (see reference).
- Know who is on the Board of Directors and their key business messages (if appropriate).

Pitfalls/Rejection points:
- Being rude to the receptionist.
- Creating a problem in the car park.
- Using recreational drugs or drinking alcohol before the interview.
- Parking in the CEO's car parking space.

Real life pitfall in action:
'Mr Confident' presented well. However he quickly came unstuck during the pre-interview icebreaker chitchat. I asked him if he had any trouble finding the location or somewhere to park. "No", he said "there were plenty of parking spaces in the car park". "Oh really", I said. 'Which car park was that?" "The small one at the front of the building" he said, with a casual air of confidence. "Didn't you see the Management Car Park sign?" I asked. "Yes", he said, "but as it was the closest one to the main reception I just parked there". "So, which park did you park in?" I asked, a little nervous about the answer. "The one marked James King, CEO". My heart sank and my blood pressure rose. The interview was then suspended while he moved his car as quickly as he could.

Experts in my network say:

> Preparation is your best friend!

-Research the job and company

-Predict questions you will be asked

-Create an Interview Q&A document that you can add to throughout your career

-Prepare a brief overview of your work history – in 5-10 minutes, not 30 minutes!

-Prepare answers to competency/behavioural questions using the STAR method*

-Prepare a separate Referees List

-Create the right impression at every contact point

-Don't forget the basics – plan to be 10 minutes early, dress appropriately and gather relevant information.

    Peta McIver
    Retired, taking time out to see
    Australia, previously IT Recruitment
    Consultant

➤ *The STAR method is a simple and effective guide to telling relevant stories about your experience and achievements. Formulate answers to questions such as "Give us an example … " or "Tell us about a time when … " using this format as a guide:

SITUATION – Set the scene e.g. the company you worked for, your role and the circumstances;

TASK – Explain the problem or what needed to de done

ACTION – Describe what you did and why

RESULT – Explain the results, outcomes or broader impacts".
>
> Peta McIver
> Retired, taking time out to see Australia, previously IT Recruitment Consultant

➤ "If you are well prepared you will:

Know your resume thoroughly including dates

Have decided on examples of work related achievements

Be able to outline relevant skills / qualities which you can bring/offer"
>
> Gaye Kidder
> Managing Director, LEC Recruitment

➤ "Preparation? It's simple. Just remember the five S's: s**t, shower, shave, suit and study".
>
> Dave Thomas,
> (Previously) Job Network Case Manager

Take a quick check-up:
- **?** Do you know the most common interview questions and have you prepared for them?
- **?** Have you put yourself in the shoes of the interviewer and anticipated their requirements?
- **?** Are you ready to mirror their prerequisites?
- **?** Are you armed with examples from your work history to tell your story?
- **?** Have you anticipated the stairs and arrived early to allow time to catch your breath?

References:
- www.forbes.com (Breathing And Your Brain)
- "Six Thinking hats" by De Bono

Notes on Chapter 6

7
IN INTERVIEW

- "Whether you think you can or think you can't, you're right". Henry Ford
- "People may hear your words, but they feel your attitude". John C. Maxwell
- "Forever is composed of nows". Emily Dickinson

By the end of this chapter you will have a better understanding of:
- ✓ The different types of interviews
- ✓ Why it is important to bring the authentic 'you' to the interview
- ✓ The unspoken language of accepting a glass of water
- ✓ How the interview is a two-way process that is informing and enquiring

Blog:
Avoid desperation, relax and be yourself.

You are the person they want. You know you are, now you just have to prove it to them. You have shown interest in the role, gone to the effort to apply and have successfully been invited to interview. All you have to do now is relax and show them the real you.

You are nervous, of course you are, and that's a good thing – it means you care.

The trick is in how you manage those nerves. Let your true personality shine through the nerves and give them something to like and then they will more easily envisage you in their team.

Accept water when it is offered as it is a token of their hospitality and a way to make you feel more at home. It can also be used to wet a dry nervous mouth and allow you a few precious seconds, whilst drinking, to compose yourself. To refuse it is insulting at some level.

Now, relax in the knowledge you are well prepared and just be you, not a forced or pretend version of you, but the authentic you.

They need to see the genuine personality of the person they're considering spending every workday with! Show them what they are buying and charm them into liking you. Find some common ground to build rapport. Be polite, don't be controversial or make arrogant or flippant remarks and always look the interviewer square in the eyes.

You have already jumped the hurdles of being suitably qualified, otherwise you would not be sitting in that chair now, so all you have to do is encourage them to believe that you are the best fit for their team and organisation.

So take another deep breath, stay in the moment, and be the best version of you!

▤ **Tables of resources for Chapter 7:**

> **Table xxii) Information sharing** recognises you are participating in a two-way process.
> **Table xxiii) Types of interviews** allows you to feel the confidence that comes from eliminating the unexpected.

▤ **Tables of resources for Chapter 7:**

> **Table xxii) Information sharing** is a list of 'information giving' and 'information gathering'.
>
> Remember that an interview is very much a two-way process. It is equally as important to gather the information you need to determine if this job is suited to you, as it is to share why you are suitable for the role. There should be lots of information being gathered about the organisation and the role, as well as industry/environment in which it operates and the make-up of the team.

| **Information giving** | • Don't be frightened to take a few seconds to pause to think about your response before you answer (this shows you have considered enough to provide relevant and appropriate information to the question and haven't just prepared stock answers)
• Answer the question that is asked, don't be worried about asking for the question again if you haven't understood it properly or are unsure of the answer (this shows your desire to give relevant information and an ability to stay on track)
• Focus on answering both parts of double-barrelled questions (this shows you can hold two thoughts at the same time and stay relevant)
• Check that you answered the question fully. If not, provide another example or more information where necessary.
• Don't volunteer too much information and keep going on and on, (this shows you can stay on task)
• Use real life examples to cement your experience, (this brings your experience to life)
• Maintain eye contact (this allows the interviewer to feel more comfortable with you)
• Answer questions to all interviewers. Don't exclude anyone.
• Sit with good posture (this shows interest and attention)
• Accept a drink if offered, water can provide you with an ice breaker and a way to keep your throat at its best. Hot drinks, on the other hand, can be awkward as they may be too hot, can spill and make a mess, cause delays whilst being made, and can be difficult to manage (particularly a cup and saucer) when you are nervous
• Participate or initiate small talk before interview begins if you have something appropriate or topical to say, (this shows you are comfortable, even if you are nervous, and demonstrates how you could fit into their team)
• 'Name-dropping' can work in your favour but only if it is considered and researched thoroughly. The danger is it can be viewed as boasting. Only use this tactic if it is of relevance and makes a good impression
• Know who works there and be armed with the info
• Drop in a relevant piece of research from the website or other available resources to show you have taken the time to check them out and know who their main competitors are |
|---|---|

	- Relax and be yourself as much as possible. They want to hire the real you, not the interview version of you who disappears once you commence work
- Be observant, notice the body language of the interviewers and how they relate to each other
- Anything to declare??
- Take your cues from the interviewer e.g. answer in a similar style and language to the interviewer to show you can easily fit in and are adaptable.
Information gathering	- Use a conversational style of questioning, rather than a grilling
- Get the balance right between talking and listening
- Listen intently to the information being given and the questions requiring answers, especially double-barrelled questions.
- Check that you have adequately answered all parts of the question
- Don't be afraid to take a list of questions with you into the interview and ask them at the end of the interview. If you refer to it and find all of them have been answered, mention it. This shows you did your preparation and if you acknowledge your questions were answered, it is a compliment to the interviewer
- Take care not to ask questions that have already been answered
- At the conclusion of the interview, exert some control by asking how long it will be until you can expect to hear a result (giving you permission to follow-up)
- Ask when the anticipated start date is
- Find out what the next step in the process is
- Are they interviewing many candidates? Did many people apply?

Tables of resources for Chapter 7 continued:

Table xxiii) Types of interviews is a list of the style, participants and stages. By identifying the possible types of interviews you can gain confidence by knowing what to expect, thereby removing the unknown quantity. Always ask what format the interview will take and who (and their titles) will be interviewing you. This allows for adequate research and preparation.

Name	What	When used:
Single	One person	
Groups	More than one person and can be up to four	
Panels	Four or five	
Distant/Remote	Phone, Skype	
Scenario	Requiring you to perform a task or act out a scenario	
Lunch/Dinner	Over a meal	
Formal/informal		
Sequential		
First		
Second		
Competency based		
Portfolio		
Interviewer:		
Human Resources		
Line Manager		
Agency		
Further Stages:		
Testing		
Medical		

Exercise/s:
🖉 Fill in the "When used" column in Table xxiii) 'Types of interviews' (use personal experience and research the remaining items).

Insider insights:
- Never speak badly about a previous employer.
- Bring examples of your work if the job is hands-on and it is appropriate to do so.
- Take control by asking permission to follow-up and find out the most appropriate way to do so – phone or email. Be sure you have the correct contact details of the interviewer.
- Be early on purpose – you learn a lot that way.
- Dry your nervous and sweating hand prior to the handshake.

Pitfalls/Rejection points:
- Not answering the questions asked but instead talking about subjects with no relevance.
- Providing very long-winded answers that inhibit the interview from progressing.
- Rude behaviour or language.
- Over-familiarity with the interviewers.
- Directing all of your eye contact to only one member of the interview panel.

Real life pitfall in action:
💣 *'Mr Uncomfortable' (around women) began the interview the way he meant to continue it – by ignoring me. Whilst he answered all of my questions, he did so by looking only at the other two interviewers, both who were male. His inability to look me in the eye, despite me being the main interviewer, was extremely off-putting and insulting.*

Experts in my network say:

> **Excerpts from "Effective interviewing"**

Be friendly, but not pushy or "chummy"

Be a problem solver

Watch your posture and your non-verbal language
    Gaye Kidder, Managing Director
    LEC Recruitment

> **Excerpt from "Interview Skills"**

Some companies may require you to complete aptitude tests / psychometric testing or personality profiles.

These are nothing to fear and can work in your favour.

Be prepared for them and it will not upset your interview.

Be honest in your responses and you will receive the best results.
    Gaye Kidder, Managing Director
    LEC Recruitment

> **Behavioural based questions:**

Where possible use 'for example' to answer these questions and refer to either past experience or your key selling points. This will give your answers depth and meaning.
    Gaye Kidder, Managing Director
    LEC Recruitment

SECTION 3. The Chapters

> **"A winning interview feels like a great conversation"**

-Bring your best attitude – leave any negative feelings and frustrations outside.

-Tick off the basics – be 10 minutes early, dress appropriately, take relevant information.

-Make a good first impression – a smile, firm handshake, direct eye contact and good presentation will get you off to a great start.

-Keep any initial warm up comments or responses brief.

-Answer questions succinctly

-Let the interviewer drive

-Ask what the next steps are

-Let the interviewer know how you are feeling about the role

-Close on a positive note".

       Peta McIver
       Retired, taking time out to see
       Australia, previously IT Recruitment
       Consultant

Take a quick check-up:

- **?** Do you understand how important it is to relax during the interview?
- **?** Do you have a list of questions prepared?
- **?** Are you checking in with your interviewers and getting feedback during the interview?
- **?** Are you giving yourself a moment to think about your answer before you start it?

References:
- biginterview.com "Face the Fear: How to Overcome Job Interview Anxiety" by Pamela Skillings
- seek.com.au "How to handle interview anxiety".

Notes on Chapter 7

8
POST INTERVIEW

- "It was character that got us out of bed, commitment that moved us into action and discipline that enabled us to follow through". Zig Ziglar
- "Actions speak louder than words". Becca Fitzpatrick
- "Good thoughts are no better than good dreams if you don't follow through". (Ralph) Waldo Emerson

By the end of this chapter you will have a better understanding of:
- ✓ How to maintain a level of control over the recruitment process
- ✓ How to prepare your referees
- ✓ Why to eat your dessert

Blog:
Thoughts to digest:

Why is it that when you eat out, not everyone has dessert?

Many say the meal isn't complete without the dessert! The same can be said for the employment process. For without the follow through that completes the *Eight Essential Elements to Employment*, you risk losing the momentum you have built up.

Remember all the good work that has taken place to get you to this point and don't waste it! You got yourself motivated, physically ready, and ensured your skills were up to date. You then prepared a resume and application letter that made you proud. You prepared for and survived the interview. So don't stop now when you can almost taste the amazing chocolate mousse or sticky date pudding!

Don't decide to go home now and miss the culmination of the culinary offerings. You need to pace yourself and not quit before the end. Finish on a high; order that dessert with ice cream *and cream* if you want.

If you walk away from an interview and simply sit around and wait for something to happen, you have lost control of the process.

SECTION 3. The Chapters

You will begin to feel impatient and rejected and will have made yourself a martyr to the possibility of failure. But failure should not be an option for you, so get busy and keep yourself in the game by being visible, professional and focused. It's time to follow-up

▤ **Table of resources for Chapter 8:**

> **Table xxiv) Things to do post-interview** when others are just waiting for the result.

▤ **Tables of resources for Chapter 8:**

> **Table xxiv) Things to do post-interview** is a list of actions you can take to help yourself stand out from other candidates, leaving a positive and professional impression on your potential employer. This list is designed to give you the best chance at success.

Action	Task
contact referees	• Call your referees to advise you have just been interviewed. Let them know by whom and ask them to advise you when they receive a call to conduct a reference check • Make sure your referees know the job title and basic duties. Discuss it with them with passion and they will get a feel for your suitability • Advise your referee about the key skills/experience the employer has identified as essential so they can include these important points in the reference check • Provide the referee with the position description of the job • Draw your referee's attention to the parallel experiences you had when working with them so they have examples in mind to call on when answering the questions • Ask your referees to think about any connections or synergies they may have with the recruiter or members of their network • All of the above make the reference check more of a conversation than a stiff process and allows the recruiter to start feeling like they know you better

send email to the interviewer	• The day after the interview, send an email thanking them and including the following: • thank them for taking the time to interview you • restate your enthusiasm about the job and the opportunity to work for their business/company/organisation • tell them you are even more enthusiastic about the role (choose whichever items are suitable for your experience) following the interview, being given the opportunity to meet them, seeing the environment, learning more about the role, having the chance to ask questions, understanding the focus of the organisation, learning about the exciting challenges on offer • say you are looking forward to being advised of the outcome • offer your availability should they require a second interview or anything else such as medical or psychometric testing, etc.
note agreed follow-up date in diary	This should have been agreed on during the interview as part of your closing remarks. Place it in your diary with an alarm so you don't miss it
follow-up on agreed date	The follow-up must be done on the day agreed, not the day before or the day after. If there is no decision made at this point do the following: • ask the reasons for the delay • ask when a decision can be expected • ask permission to follow-up again at an appropriate time (usually two weeks) • thank the Recruiter for their time and acknowledge you know how busy they are • try to engage in conversation if appropriate, otherwise, respect their time is valuable and keep to the point
note new agreed follow-up date in diary	Place the date in your diary with an alarm so you don't miss it
follow-up on agreed date	The follow-up *must* be done on the day agreed. If there is still no decision at this point, repeat the steps listed above

negotiate an offer	Things to discuss at point of offer: • salary (this would ordinarily have been discussed during the interview and if the Recruiter is doing their job well there will be no surprises) • package (all relevant items in the package e.g. company car, parking, conditions and benefits • start date (this is when you mention any holidays you have already booked, if you haven't already done so during the interview) • declare disability (if you have a disability/medical condition that may be affected by performing the duties of the job you may wish to declare it, this is not compulsory and is personal choice) N.B. This is general advice and may not be the best advice for some specific conditions. Seek further advice from medical professionals or your professional support network.
accept an offer	You can accept an offer verbally over the phone based on the information provided in the offer. This is often followed-up with a written confirmation in the form of a letter of offer and contract, to be signed prior to commencement.
plan commencement	Starting a new job is a big deal and should be planned for. Consider the following: • plot the best route to work • allow enough time for traffic • determine what time your alarm needs to be set • have a backup to the alarm (to help you settle into your new pattern) • prepare the night before so there is less to do in the morning • advise your friends that you won't be available on your mobile during working hours • plan your meals for the week on the weekend. Doing the shopping and some preparation of food will make lunchtimes easier and more cost effective, and your dinner times less time consuming and tiring • organise your work clothes/shoes, etc. • find out ahead of the start day where to park or the best alternative transport methods • clear your social schedule for the first few weeks to allow for settling in and absorbing new information • focus on being well rested and feeling comfortable

enact commencement plan	• don't expect too much from yourself in the first week • record important information so you are not asking questions about information you have already been given • make a note of the names of your team members • if you are given a mentor, make the most of the opportunity • take notes during the induction if you are not provided with handouts • know who to go to with your questions • don't sit back and wait for things. Use your initiative and ask the appropriate people if you need help
expect retention	Understand that a new job can be a lot to deal with and go easy on yourself. Consider the following: • new environment • new people • new expectations • trying to fit in • new terminology and every workplace uses its own specific set of jargon
Stay alert and keep a look out for anyone trying to 'move your cheese'*! *This reference relates to a book listed at the end of this chapter. Look for the 'writing on the wall'. It is often hidden, but if you look hard enough you'll see it.	long-term happiness at work, once achieved, may be dependent on external forces such as: • the organisation's direction • the economic climate • social change • new inventions • profitability of your industry • mechanisation of jobs • casualisation of the workforce • political changes • tax laws • other laws • disasters • unforeseen situations • changes in moral views to your industry • nanotechnology • advances in science • new medical breakthroughs … and many more Keep researching, stay current with your knowledge and never stop being curious!

Exercise/s:

🖉 Regularly review your position, become business savvy and don't let anyone move your cheese! (This reference relates to the situation whereby you find yourself in changed circumstances that may have been predicted had you been more aware of the bigger picture and poised for change.)

Insider insights:

👍 Send a thank you note to the person who interviewed you in the form of an email. This, when worded appropriately, will leave a great impression and increase your chances of being seen favourably.

👍 When following-up with the interviewer, do so according to the agreed schedule and don't be too pushy or become a nuisance. It can be a fine line.

Pitfalls/Rejection points:

✋ Don't get your name on the lips and minds of the interviewer for being a nuisance.

✋ Not being proactive, sitting back and waiting for a decision that isn't coming, then taking out your frustration on the recruiter.

✋ Following-up too quickly, too often and/or in inappropriate ways.

Real life pitfall in action:

💣 *'Mr Enthusiastic', the internal candidate who applied for every job that was advertised irrespective of what it was, rang to check on the progress of his application several times a week. His follow-up became so incessant that it even prevented me from buying my lunch at the staff canteen for fear of being bailed up every time he saw me! He started to earn a reputation around the place – the type of reputation you don't want!*

Experts in my network say:

> "The interview is not the end of the selection process!
>
> -Initial interview feedback is key to gauging interest and can influence the result
>
> -A post-interview email confirming your interest can be well received but isn't essential
>
> -A follow-up email or call to check progress is acceptable
>
> -The next steps could include a 2nd or 3rd interviews or homework tasks
>
> -Roll with the process and be patient
>
> -Ask for feedback
>
> -Not getting the job doesn't mean you have lost or failed".
>
>> Peta McIver
>> Retired, taking time out to see Australia, previously IT Recruitment Consultant

> "Close on a positive note – no matter how you feel about the interview, make a professional exit with a handshake and thank the interviewer for their time and the opportunity".
>> Peta McIver
>> Retired, taking time out to see Australia, previously IT Recruitment Consultant

> "Not getting the job doesn't mean you have lost or failed – There are always positives to take away. At the very least, you have expanded your network and developed your interviewing skills".
> Peta McIver
> Retired, taking time out to see Australia, previously IT Recruitment Consultant

Take a quick check-up:
- **?** Have you laid the foundation to keep some control over the recruitment process?
- **?** Are you feeling confident that you have done all you could to be successful?
- **?** Are you expecting retention in your new job?

References:
- *"The Art of Happiness at work"* by Dalai Lama & Dr. Howard Cutler
- *"Who Moved My Cheese?"* by Spencer Johnson

This simple little book has been mentioned before in the relevant chapter, but it is a good thought to leave you with.

In my opinion, everybody should read this and learn the life lessons contained within. Sometimes it is the smallest of things that make the biggest difference – this book certainly made a difference to me.

Notes on Chapter 8

SECTION 3. The Chapters

> **Table xxv) Summary of Eight Essential Elements to Employment** recaps the steps to take when seeking employment. By following each element within the chapters you will see the logical progression from wanting a job to securing one.

Attitude check (See Chapter 1)	• Remember to expect success.
Presentation (See Chapter 2)	• Be the best version of you.
Choose the role (See Chapter 3)	• Are you desperate to work and will do anything to work or are you making a career choice? It is important to differentiate between a survival job and a career job • *Only* apply for jobs you would accept • *Only* apply for suitable jobs. Don't use a scatter gun approach, applying for anything and everything, as this will reduce your chances of success and increase your frustration.
Look in the right places (See Chapter 4)	• Aim for the role you desire.
Job search routine (See Chapter 5)	• Accept that searching for a job is currently your full-time job (if unemployed) • Establish which career websites are relevant and check them daily • Check in with regularly with recruitment companies where appropriate.
Preparation, research (See Chapter 6)	• Be market savvy! Who is your competition? • How can you best compete?
Perform at interview (See Chapter 7)	• Relax and show your personality.
Follow through (See Chapter 8)	• Impress with a professional follow through.
Go for it!	

SECTION 4. The Lists

Definitions

Abbreviations

Resources

Quotes

Definitions:

Word	Meaning
Acronyms	Word or name formed as an abbreviation
Appropriate	Suitable or proper given the particular circumstances
Cadence	Rhythmic pattern of writing
Career job	A job that allows progression or fits into a planned pathway
Chronological	A record of events showing the order in which they occurred
Contract of Employment	Oral or written agreement specifying terms and conditions of employment
Employment Contract	Oral or written agreement specifying terms and conditions of employment
Jobactive	The Commonwealth Government networks that assist unemployed clients on benefits
Job Guide	Prepared and updated annually by Australian Government, detailing job titles with extensive information and data
Job Network	Previous name for Jobactive
Mission Statement	A written statement of an organisation's core purpose and focus
Maslow's hierarchy of needs	Maslow (an American Psychologist) stated that people are motivated to achieve certain needs and that some needs take precedence. See pyramid depiction online
Nanotechnology	Manipulation of matter that is impacting many professions
Op Shops	Opportunity Shops are retail outlet selling low cost clothing, shoes, bags and accessories
Per diem	Each day
Pro rata	Part of the full amount

Salutations	Greeting used at beginning and end of letter
Selection Criteria	A list of questions or statements that should be addressed if requested, usually found on the Position Description
Standard Letters	Letters used by recruiters to advise you of the status of your application N.B. Use of a "Standard letter" is common business practice for organisations to advise candidates that their application has been rejected. These letters signal the end of the recruitment process.
Survival job	A job taken purely to earn money, often as a short-term plan until something better comes along
Talk the talk	Speak convincingly about something in a way that impresses and shows you understand the topic
Vision Board	A visual representation of how you want things to be
Writing on the wall	A clear indication of failure or disaster

Abbreviations:

Acronym	Expanded
AA	Affirmative Action
ABN	Australian Business Number
ACSF	Australian Core Skills Framework is a tool that assists the description of an individual's performance in the five core skills of learning, reading, writing, oral communication & numeracy

ACT	Australian Capital Territory Year 12 Certificate
AIDA Model	Attention, Interest, Desire, Action, used in Marketing and Advertising to develop effective communication strategies
AQF	Australian Qualifications Framework, designed by the Australian Government to ensure consistency in Australian education
ASCO	Australian Standard Classifications of Occupations
ATO	Australian Taxation Office
AWA	Australian Workplace Agreement
CALD	Culturally & Linguistically Diverse
CEO	Chief Executive Officer
COO	Chief Operating Officer
CPI	Consumer Price Index
CV	Curriculum Vitae (also known as a resume)
DOB	Date of Birth
DSP	Disability Support Pension
EEO	Equal Employment Opportunity
ER	Employee Relations
EQ	Emotional Quotient
HR	Human Resources
HRD	Human Resources Development
HRM	Human Resources Management
HSC	Higher School Certificate (NSW)
IQ	Intelligence Quotient
IR	Industrial Relations
JP	Job Plan, prepared by Jobactive Member and individualised for each client

SECTION 4. The Lists

JS	Job search
LOO	Letter of Offer
MBTI	Myer-Briggs Type Indicator
MO	Mutual obligation
MOU	Memorandum of Understanding
MRI	Magnetic Resonance Imaging, a medical test
NEIS	New Enterprise Incentive Scheme
NSA	Newstart Allowance
NTCET	Northern Territory Certificate of Education & Training
OH&S/OHS	Occupational Health & Safety
OTE	Opportunities to earn
PD	Position Description (Human Resources)
PD	Professional Development (Teachers etc.)
QCE	Queensland Certificate of Education
SACE	South Australian Certificate of Education
SMART	Specific, Measureable, Attainable, Relevant & Time Bound. A way of measuring goals.
TAFE	Technical and Further Education
TEMP	Temporary Employee
TCE	Tasmanian Certificate of Education
VCE	Victorian Certificate of Education
VCAL	Victorian Certificate of Applied Learning
VTA	Victorian Tertiary Admissions Centre
WACE	Western Australian Certificate of Education
WftD	Work for the Dole

WHS	Harmonisation of OHS Laws (except VIC & WA)

📰 **Resources:**

Chart	Item	Resources for:	Location
a)	Flowchart: Eight Essential Elements to Employment	Individual & Business Professional & Consultant	Section 2 The Elements

Table	Item	Resources for:	Location
i)	The Recruitment Process	Individual & Consultant	
ii)	Adjectives for Rocking Resume	Individual & Consultant	
iii)	The Recruitment Process	Business Professional	
iv)	Scoring candidates in interview	Business Professional	
v)	Goal setting		Ch1
vi)	Personal hygiene		Ch2
vii)	Personal presentation		Ch2
viii)	Choose a career		Ch3
ix)	Employability skills		Ch3
x)	Personal attributes		Ch3
xi)	Upskill yourself		Ch3
xii)	Transferrable skills		Ch3
xiii)	Where to find jobs		Ch4

SECTION 4. The Lists

xiv)	Amazing Application inclusions		Ch4
xv)	Structure of Amazing Application		Ch4
xvi)	Ways to stand out		Ch4
xvii)	Selection Criteria should be:		Ch4
xviii)	Format of a Rocking Resume		Ch5
ixx)	Structure of a Rocking Resume		Ch5
xx)	Turn weaknesses into strengths		Ch6
xxi)	Record of applications		Ch6
xxii)	Information sharing		Ch7
xxiii)	Types of interviews		Ch7
xxiv)	Things to do post-interview		Ch8
xxv)	Summary of Eight Essential Elements to Employment	Individual & Consultant	

153

> **💬 Quotes:**
> In most cases, the 'known for' column details one or two things the person being quoted was primarily known for. In many cases, however, there is a longer list of their achievements. You are encouraged to look them up, especially if the particular quote resonates with you. You may benefit from doing some further reading about any of the interesting and diverse people included in this book.

Who's quote	Known for	Page No
Brian Tracy	American Author	xi, 51, 54
Disney	The Walt Disney Company	46
Lao Tzu	Ancient Chinese Philosopher and Writer	46
Turia Pitt	Australian Author and Motivational Speaker	46
Theodore Roosevelt	American Politician	54
C. S. Lewis	British Novelist and Poet	66
George Bernard Shaw	Irish Playwright	66
Confucius	Chinese Philosopher	66
Louisa May Alcott	American Novelist and Poet	80
Hans Hofmann	American Painter	80
Lemony Snicket	Pen name of American Writer Daniel Handler	80
Aristotle	Ancient Greek Philosopher	94
Truman Capote	American Novelist	94
Leonardo da Vinci	Italian Painter	94
George R. R. Martin	American Novelist	112

Benjamin Franklin	Founding Father of United States	112
Neil Armstrong	American Astronaut	112
Henry Ford	American Industrialist	124
John C. Maxwell	American Author	124
Emily Dickinson	American Poet	124
Zig Ziglar	American Author and Motivational Speaker	136
Becca Fitzpatrick	American Author	136
(Ralph) Waldo Emerson	American Poet	136

SECTION 5. The Next Step

Ways to work with me:

The Individual
- Resume
- Application
- Resume check-up (diagnostics & treatment for DIY)
- Employment Coaching
- Career counselling
- Customised Assistance

The Business Professional
- Application receipt, screening, shortlisting
- Application referrals/recommendations
- Reference checking
- Position Descriptions
- Procedures/Policies
- Customised Assistance

The Consultant
- Employment Coaching
- Customised Assistance

*Schedule of charges is available upon request.

Contact:
Pauline Visser Employment Coaching
+61 488 788 723
Email: paulinevisserec@gmail.com
www.paulinevisserec.net
FB: Pauline Visser Employment Coaching
Linkedin.com/in/pauline-visser-640ab557

Notes

Notes

Notes

Notes

www.ingramcontent.com/pod-product-compliance
Lightning Source LLC
Chambersburg PA
CBHW071449080526
44587CB00014B/2048